# Praise for *Cheetah* Negotiations

"As a busy litigation and trial attorney, I recognize the need for negotiation skills to achieve the best results for my clients. *Cheetah Negotiations* provides these skills. The tips and techniques contained in the book far surpass anything taught in law school, but their usefulness extends well beyond the legal setting. This book presents the reader with the necessary tools to succeed in any type of negotiations. "

— Matthew S. Hirsch, Esq.
Trumbull, Connecticut

"Negotiations are critical to business success, and are often the Achilles heel for many of us. The tactics presented in *Cheetah Negotiations* gave me insight into both my professional and personal negotiations. After reading *Cheetah Negotiations*, I feel better prepared and more confident to handle negotiations at any level."

— Carey Earle, CEO, Green Apple Marketing
New York, New York

"This book takes a look at more than negotiation tactics. It looks at the human behaviors and personalities that drive them. Reading *Cheetah Negotiations* gave me a firm grasp of these issues and some practical instruction on how to apply them. As the owner of a consulting business, I am constantly in negotiations, from large contracts to everyday project trade-offs. The concepts I learned are quickly becoming second nature, which helps me to operate at peak effectiveness and efficiency."

— Sarah Howarth, Owner, Shore to Shore Software
Gloucester, Massachusetts

"This book helps you think through negotiations as a logical process. It shows you how to systematically plan, bargain, and close the deal. They actually teach you how to make negotiations fun! Let's face it, life is full of all sorts of negotiations and personalities. Cheetah provides you with the knowledge and tools to make you successful at the art of negotiations! After reading this book, I am confident that I can get everything that I deserve!"

— Susan Tague, PMP, Project Manager
Bloomfield, Connecticut


"I recommend this book to my clients who are serious about improving their financial situations. Whether you need to negotiate for a pay raise or grow a business, Cheetah Negotiation skills are the key to financial success."

— Liz Charron, Owner, Reservoir Financial
Mansfield Center, Connecticut


"This book takes an in-depth look at not just negotiation tactics, but at the human personalities and behaviors that drive them. Knowing this is essential to successful negotiation. Reading *Cheetah Negotiations* gave me a firm understanding of these factors, as well as great instructions on how to apply them to any negotiation situation."

— Dennis McClintick, PMP, MBA, SAP Programmer
Cuyahoga Falls, Ohio

# *Cheetah*
# NEGOTIATIONS

**Book Two**
*The Cheetah Success Series*

*Cheetah*
# NEGOTIATIONS

## How to Get What You Want, Fast

*Michelle LaBrosse, PMP*
*Linda Lansky, PMP*

**MAKLAF PRESS**
Carson City,

Cheetah Negotiations
by Michelle LaBrosse, PMP and Linda Lansky, PMP
Published by Maklaf Press LLC.
502 N. Division St., Carson City, NV  89703
A Division of MAKLAF Holding Inc.
www.cheetahlearning.com

    Notice: This publication contains the opinions and ideas of the authors. It is intended to provide helpful and informative material on the subject matters cov-ered. It is not meant to replace the advice of an attorney. The authors and publisher specifically disclaim any responsibility for any liability, loss, or risk, personal or otherwise, which is incurred as a consequence, directly or indirectly, of the use and/or application of any of the contents of this book.

    Post-It, Slinky, Myers-Briggs, and all other brand, product, service, and company names are trademarks of their respective holders. Reference to a product, service, or company does not imply recommendation, approval, affiliation, or sponsorship of that product, service, or company by either the authors or MAKLAF Press.

MAKLAF Press books are available at special quantity discounts to use as premiums and sales promotions, or for use in corporate training programs. For more information, please write to the Director of Sales, MAKLAF Press 502 N. Division Street, Carson City, Nevada 89703, or contact your local bookstore.

*Cover and interior design by Pneuma Books, LLC.* Visit www.pneumabooks.com

**Publisher's Cataloging-in-Publication Data**
(Prepared by The Donohue Group, Inc.)

LaBrosse, Michelle.
    Cheetah negotiations : how to get what you want, fast / Michelle LaBrosse, Linda Lansky.

    p. : ill. ; cm. -- (Cheetah success series ; Book 2)
    Includes bibliographical references and index.
    ISBN: 0-9761749-2-8

1. Negotiation--Psychological aspects--Handbooks, manuals, etc. 2. Negotiation in business. 3. Interpersonal communication. I. Lansky, Linda. II. Title.

BF637.N4 L33 2005
302.3                                                    LCCN: 2005921685

10  09  08  07  06  05                          6  5  4  3  2  1

*To my children — the two best negotiators on the planet!*
~Michelle LaBrosse~


*To my family, who believe I can do anything*
~Linda Lansky~

# Contents

# Preface

*W*hy did I write this book? Throughout my life I have been able to achieve my goals faster than most everyone on the planet. I started thinking about the core reasons for my successes and identified two key strategies that I have consistently used. The first is to help other people get what they want. When I focused on what it was other people wanted, I got what I wanted. For example, I wanted to attend Syracuse University. It was an expensive school, and I had five siblings all of college age with two parents who were public school teachers. The U.S. Government wanted military officers who were majoring in engineering, and they were willing to give full scholarships to people who would serve in the military after they completed their college degree. Voila, I gave the U.S. Government what it wanted, I got what I wanted.

But giving people what they want isn't the only strategy that made me successful. The second key strategy was developing and using easy systems to achieve my goals. Lots of people have great ideas and great intentions. But they lack the wherewithal to create a process that they can easily follow day in and day out that enables them to quickly achieve their goals. So, I started to question, just how do I go about helping other people achieve what they want so I can achieve what I want?

That is what led my co-author Linda Lansky and I to create the Cheetah Negotiations process. We had discovered the secret to getting what I want fast is to take the time to really get to know what other people want — to find out their personal issues and understand what they need. Most of the time, there are many subconscious, unspoken expectations. Despite wide variations in people's personal styles that could make negotiating very tough, I have developed ways to consistently communicate in a way that creates positive, solutions-oriented explorations. This enables the achievement of shared and individual objectives. I don't expect or wait for others to be on the same level as I am with negotiations. It is of no consequence if they are not into a win-win negotiation strategy. What matters at the end of the day is whether I helped them get what they wanted because ultimately it will help me get what I want, fast. And I do this day in and day out with methodical precision.

The key to sharing the Cheetah Negotiations method with the world was the efforts of my co-author Linda Lansky. Linda recognized the process that I had made a subconscious part of my day-to-day existence over twenty years of practicing it. As a detached observer, Linda was able to pull the process out and see it in all its simplicity. Linda wanted to write a book. I wanted to share the two fundamental elements of my success with the world. We negotiated a partnership and away we went. First we created an on-line course to teach what we now call Cheetah Negotiations, and then we penned this book. The partnership has given both of us what we want.

You can achieve your goals faster than you've ever imagined. The Cheetah Negotiations process might work for you. Or you might discover that there are elements of this process that work successfully for you, but you need to do things just a little differently. The main thing to remember is that you can achieve what you set out to achieve in life, fast. You don't need to wait years to pursue your goals or to get what you want. You can do it, now. There is a tremendous bonus in addition to getting what you want. What you will learn by helping other people get what they want, so you can get what you want, is worth far more than anything you will achieve along the way. Welcome to the journey of a well-lived, successful life.

~Michelle LaBrosse, PMP

# *Acknowledgments*

As with any great work, numerous people helped us bring this work to print. Pam Peacock, PMP, took up the banner with the publishing process. It was with her diligence that our team completed the book and got it published. Alexis Bohan spent many hours editing and re-editing the manuscript. Sharene Santos worked on a variety of the graphic elements. Michelle's children spent not one, but two, of their vacations with Mom and Linda Lansky in Hawaii while they worked on the course and then the book. Barbara Sleeper took the first shift of book development during our second writing trip to Hawaii. And there are the hundreds of our students who have verified this process works — including one of our first students, Barbara McClintick, who used the Cheetah Negotiation concepts to negotiate a job for herself with Cheetah Learning. Thank you all for the role you played in making this work available to the public.

# *Cheetah*
# NEGOTIATIONS

# INTRODUCTION

*heetah Negotiations* is a way for you to get what you want, fast. In this book we present a process of efficiently preparing for the many styles of negotiations you encounter daily. The process ensures you negotiate with other people fairly, in a way that helps you develop long-term, growing relationships. With this approach, every party in a negotiation will get what they want, fast. The more you can help other people get what they want, the more you will create opportunities that will continue to rapidly expand your own success story.

This book is designed to walk you through the steps of the Cheetah Negotiations process. Each step might seem simple, but that's exactly what makes this technique so fast and effective. The more you go through the process, the more it will become a habit, and the easier it will be to apply to more complex negotiations. In the beginning, however, you need to pay close attention to all the steps — it's the way of the cheetah after all!

There are four sections in this book, and each section focuses on a different step within the process. In each section there are two to three chapters depending on the steps within each process section. For each chapter we present the main concepts and ideas along with opportunities to practice these concepts. Each chapter finishes with sections asking you to *Reflect* and *Act* based upon the ideas presented. Practicing gives you the opportunity to explore how to put the theory to use in your own environment and to check your work against examples we provide. We recommend buying a notebook with thirty to forty pages of blank paper to record your results of the activities. Reflecting prompts you to think about what you experienced and what you still need to learn. When you reflect on what you experienced and attach an emotion to how you felt about what you learned, you remember it better and have an easier time recalling your key learning points. Finally, you create a plan to act, describing how you're going to apply what you just learned. When you take specific action on what you have just learned, it becomes part of who you are and you will be on your way to faster, more effective negotiations.

## CHEETAH NEGOTIATIONS PROCESS

As Shakespeare so eloquently penned, "All the world's a stage, and all the men and women merely players. They have their exits and entrances, and one man in his time plays many parts" (Bartlett's, 198). The Cheetah Negotiations process uses the theatre as an allegory for the different steps you'll walk through in learning to become a better negotiator. Much preparation goes on before an opening night on stage, and the quality of that preparation plays a big role in the success or failure of the performance. Negotiations are the same.

The sections of this book outline the steps in the Cheetah Negotiations process:

## PREPARING FOR NEGOTIATIONS

Once you go through this negotiation process several times, it will become rote and you'll whiz through it with your eyes closed. The time that you invest now in learning the basics will reap you huge benefits in making all of your negotiations more effective.

## JUMP-STARTING NEGOTIATIONS PREPARATIONS

You do have the ability to get what you want, fast. If you're clear about what you want, willing to work with others to help them get what they want, and know how to follow these simple steps on a consistent basis, you will find that you can get what you want, fast, time after time after time after time. You'll move like a cheetah.

*Section One*
# The Cast of Characters

The first part of successful and speedy negotiations is to understand yourself, your motivations, and the cast of characters with whom you're negotiating. It's as if "the world's a stage, and all the men and women merely players." To really move fast in your negotiations, you need to know just who these characters are. As Pope said, "Know then thyself, presume not God to scan; The proper study of mankind is man" (Bartlett's, 311). Or, as Plato said, "Trees and fields tell me nothing: men are my teachers" (Bartlett's, 311).

*Once was a person called me*
*Who wanted to know who to be*
*So I took the test*
*You know the rest*
*Now I'm as happy as can be*

# Know Thyself: What Is Your Role?

*I*n this chapter, you will learn how to study the cast of characters to speed up your negotiations. The intent of this chapter and the next is to help you start gathering information about the different personality types that exist — and how they play out in your negotiation theatre. The theory behind personality types is based on the work of Swiss psychologist Carl Jung and, more recently, Isabel Myers and Katharine Briggs, who developed the Myers-Briggs Type Indicator® (MBTI) psychological instrument to identify sixteen distinctly different types of personality.

There are four components, or dimensions, that make up a personality type. They are:

1. How people are energized
2. What type of information they naturally notice and remember
3. How they make decisions

4. How they like to organize the world around them

As you can see, each of these dimensions deals with an important aspect of life, which is why personality type provides such accurate insights into our own behavior and the behavior of others.

Lao-tzu said, "He who knows others is wise; He who knows himself is enlightened" (Bartlett's, 59). This expression is particularly true with regard to learning about personality types. Therefore, your first objective is to understand the type concepts well enough to be able to accurately identify your own type. This tool is designed to help people better understand themselves and others so that they can communicate more successfully.

Once you understand your own type, you can start to read other people's types. With this information, you can move onto the next section where you can best set the stage based on the cast of characters in each negotiation.

## YOU AS THE LEADING CHARACTER

In our online *Cheetah Negotiations* class, our students take an online assessment to discover their innate strengths and personal challenges for negotiating in the various roles they play day to day in professional and personal situations. This assessment is a modified Myers-Briggs personality type assessment. If you already know your Myers-Briggs personality type, find it below to read about your innate negotiation strengths and weaknesses. If you do not know your Myers-Briggs personality type, you can visit www.personalitytype.com and complete the assessment found there, or you can do the assessment here that is adapted from the book *Do What You Are* by Barbara Barron-Tieger and Paul Tieger.

We provide a simplified personality assessment here based on the four dimensions, but we recommend you go online and do a more comprehensive survey to get a more accurate assessment. Consider where you fit into each dimension, and you can generally figure out your personality type. Putting the four letters together will give you your type.

- **E or I** — Extrovert (E) or Introvert (I) relates to how you are energized. Do you get excited and animated around others (E)? Or do you prefer to be off on your own (I)?

- **N or S** — Intuitive (N) or Sensory (S) relates to what you focus on in your environment. Where do you place your focus? Do you look at "what could be" (N)? Or do you see "what is" (S)? People who fit the "N" classification are "idea" people and the people who fit the "S" classification are driven by "real" facts and data.

- **T or F** — Thinker (T) or Feeler (F) relates to how you make decisions. Reflect on how you make decisions. Do you make decisions impersonally, prefacing comments with "I think..." (T)? Or do you make decisions based on your own values, sometimes prefacing comments with "I feel..." (F)?

- **J or P** — Judging (J) or Perceiving (P) relates to how you choose to live. Notice the state of your desk. Do you prefer to keep your desk neat and tidy (i.e., very structured) (J)? Or do you prefer to keep it more spontaneously organized (i.e., very flexible) (P)? People who fit the "J" classification prefer an orderly life and are happiest when matters are settled. People who fit the "P" classification prefer to be spontaneous and are happiest when their lives are more flexible.

Now that you have determined your personality type (either through an online assessment or the adaptation provided here), you can gain valuable insight on how it plays a role in your life.

Next we will examine all sixteen personality types' innate negotiation strengths and blind spots. Find your personality type from this list and review your strengths and blind spots.

## INTJ

### Possible Strengths
- Solves problems creatively; capable of developing original solutions
- Thinks strategically; can appreciate the big picture and think several moves ahead
- Thoughtful and deliberate; considers information carefully before taking action
- Competent, knowledgeable, and prepared; does their homework
- Logical; evaluates information objectively

### Possible Blind Spots
- May not spend the necessary time to establish rapport or develop relationships
- May cause confusion by not communicating clearly
- May exhibit impatience with those who don't understand their points immediately
- May tend to be inflexible and difficult to persuade once they've made up their mind
- May be unrealistic, especially in regard to how others will feel about a specific issue or proposal

## ENTP

### Possible Strengths
- Solves problems creatively; sees possibilities and options

- Understands others' motives and how to reach them; extremely perceptive about people
- Can shift gears quickly when necessary; quick and flexible
- Can be very entertaining and persuasive; charming and charismatic
- Can absorb and integrate concepts and information quickly

## Possible Blind Spots
- May not prepare themselves adequately; often prefers to wing it
- May not listen attentively
- May not be very interested in details and specifics of issues
- May be unreliable and unrealistic and promise more than they can deliver
- May have trouble committing to a decision and performing necessary follow-through

# INTP

## Possible Strengths
- Understands complexities and nuances of issues
- Competent and knowledgeable about subjects that interest them
- Solves problems creatively; often gifted at devising innovative options
- Confident in their abilities and often communicates that to others
- Able to strategize brilliantly

## Possible Blind Spots
- May not communicate clearly; what makes sense to them may be confusing to others

- May be impatient with others who are not as quick or smart as they are
- May have unrealistic expectations of what is achievable within a certain time period
- May not always prepare adequately and may lack timely follow-through
- May not be able to respond in the moment because they do their best thinking in private

## ESTJ

### Possible Strengths
- Realistic; focuses on practical solutions to problems
- Responsible, trustworthy, and fair-minded; communicates reliability and stability
- Organized, well prepared, and efficient
- Makes logical and objective decisions; doesn't take things too personally
- Pays attention to important details; accurate with facts

### Possible Blind Spots
- May have difficulty establishing rapport and accepting others' values
- May make decisions before considering all options
- May be unable or unwilling to consider nontraditional approaches or solutions
- May not be flexible or adaptable enough when they need to change their positions
- May be unable to fully grasp the long-term implications of current actions

## ISTJ

### Possible Strengths
- Extremely attentive to details and accurate with facts
- Organized, hardworking, prepared, and efficient
- Makes thoughtful, practical decisions
- Realistic expectations with regard to resources, process, and so forth
- Good powers of concentration; single-minded and assertive

### Possible Blind Spots
- May not be comfortable with new or untried methods; needs concrete proof
- May be particularly resistant to change the way things have been done in the past
- May not read opponents well; may miss important information about what they are thinking
- May have difficulty shifting gears or changing directions quickly
- May be unable or unwilling to focus on future needs and implications of negotiations

## ESFJ

### Possible Strengths
- Warm and friendly; good at making people feel comfortable
- Organized, prepared, practical, and efficient
- Responsible and reliable; has good command of important facts and details
- Driven to closure, which can expedite the process
- Loyal to organizations' values and people; will work hard to do right by them

### Possible Blind Spots

- May be easily, though inadvertently, offended, which may dampen their enthusiasm
- May find adversarial aspects of negotiations too unharmonious and stressful
- May be unable or unwilling to explore possibilities they see as impractical or unrealistic
- May be in so much of a hurry to conclude negotiations that they miss important ancillary issues
- Tends to overlook their own needs because of their desire to please other people

## ISFJ

### Possible Strengths

- Meticulous and thorough; possesses impressive command of relevant facts and details
- Warm and welcoming; makes opponents feel comfortable and unthreatened
- Organized and efficient; comfortable following prescribed process
- Great depth of focus; able to stay on task and explore issues in depth
- Reliable and trustworthy; inspires opponents to have confidence in their honesty and integrity

### Possible Blind Spots

- May be uncomfortable considering new ideas, especially if they have yet to be demonstrated successful elsewhere
- May find adversarial aspect of negotiations too unharmonious and stressful
- May become overwhelmed when required to juggle several ideas or proposals at the same time

- May have difficulty predicting future impact of current proposals
- May become intimidated by more aggressive opponents

## ESTP

### Possible Strengths
- Tends to enjoy whatever they're doing, so they make the process fun
- Adaptable; can shift gears quickly; especially good in a crisis
- Good at applying practical solutions based on past observations and experiences
- Can be tough but friendly at the same time; not likely to get upset or intimidated
- Comfortable taking calculated risks but also has good common sense

### Possible Blind Spots
- May not have done the necessary homework or prepared enough in advance
- May not see opportunities and possibilities that don't exist at the moment
- May be easily distracted from the task at hand
- May be seen as too cavalier and not taken seriously enough
- May have trouble following the "rules," or procedures, of negotiations if they feel excessively restricted by them

## ISTP

### Possible Strengths
- Willing to take calculated risks
- Excellent memory for important factual information
- Stays clear-headed and cool in a crisis situation

- Good at finding practical solutions; can exercise good common sense
- Adaptable and flexible; can shift gears quickly

### Possible Blind Spots
- May be very uncommunicative; uncomfortable engaging in small talk/rapport building
- May be blunt; may not recognize the value or need for tact and diplomacy
- May not be particularly perceptive about what makes others tick
- May not prepare adequately
- May get bored or lack patience if dealing with complicated or abstract concepts

## ESFP

### Possible Strengths
- Positive and upbeat attitude; makes the negotiating process enjoyable and fun
- Able to adapt well to change; can shift gears quickly
- Genuine fondness for people that makes others comfortable
- Very observant; can assess situations and resources realistically
- Desires to achieve a win-win situation, which fosters cooperation

### Possible Blind Spots
- May accept things at face value and miss underlying issues and their meaning
- May be too accommodating in a desire to promote harmonious relationships

- May become defensive when receiving feedback they perceive as negative
- May become easily distracted and lose focus
- May not excel at thinking strategically

## ENFJ

### Possible Strengths
- Puts people at ease and makes them feel comfortable; engaging and enthusiastic
- Driven to come up with a satisfactory solution; goal oriented
- Can communicate their positions clearly with passion and conviction; articulate
- Perceptive, sensitive, and accommodating to others' needs
- Likes win-win situations; tries to create a harmonious atmosphere

### Possible Blind Spots
- May give up too much for the sake of maintaining interpersonal harmony
- May become prickly if offended by opponents' comments or style
- May become inflexible if required to compromise one of their values
- May be too idealistic and not pragmatic enough
- May reach an agreement prematurely, without considering all important facts

## INFJ

### Possible Strengths
- Creative; good at thinking outside the box
- Has great integrity and commands respect from opponents

- Listens well; perceptive about people
- Considers options thoughtfully, without rushing to judgment
- Organized, prepared, and driven to meet their goals

### Possible Blind Spots
- May present solutions that are not realistic or practical enough to work
- May not communicate their ideas and vision simply or clearly enough
- May become inflexible and stubborn when proposals that reflect one of their important values is challenged or dismissed
- May have difficulty juggling several options/issues at the same time
- May lack objectivity and take negotiations too personally

## ENFP

### Possible Strengths
- Very perceptive about others; good at reading people
- Sees the big picture and can usually generate many creative options
- Establishes rapport easily and maintains friendly relationships
- Good at asking the right questions to learn what they need to know
- Open-minded to new possibilities and options

### Possible Blind Spots
- May get swept up with creative but unrealistic and/or impractical ideas
- May be too accommodating; may give away too much, too early in the process

- May not pay close attention to the details and may lose sight of priorities
- May seem flighty or scattered and make unrealistic promises
- May back down too quickly when confronted by strong opponents

## INFP

### Possible Strengths

- Very perceptive about others; good at making people feel comfortable
- Excellent listeners; possesses good communication skills
- Deeply committed to issues they believe in strongly; passionate; excels at advocacy
- Solves problems creatively
- Works hard to come up with satisfying solutions; seeks win-win situations

### Possible Blind Spots

- May be too idealistic and not realistic enough about what is achievable
- May have difficulty compromising on big issues
- May be easily offended and lose enthusiasm or the desire to continue the relationship
- May lack ability to evaluate issues and positions objectively
- May not be assertive enough; may be perceived as weak and vulnerable

## ENTJ

### Possible Strengths

- Exudes confidence in their positions and abilities

- Knowledgeable about issues; well prepared and organized
- Thinks strategically; views negotiation process as a chess match
- Makes logical arguments; supports their positions with compelling reasons
- Highly competitive and assertive

### Possible Blind Spots
- May be perceived as arrogant and superior
- May be overly aggressive and intimidate opponents
- May not have the skill or take the time to try and develop relationships
- May lack sensitivity to or perceptiveness about what is most important to others
- May be impatient with process and push for closure prematurely

## ISFP

### Possible Strengths
- Able to make people feel comfortable and valued
- Practical and realistic; good common sense
- Good knowledge of the details that are important to people
- Flexible; willing to take calculated risks
- Strong sense of loyalty to their ideals and organizations

### Possible Blind Spots
- May lack assertiveness due to their strong desire to avoid conflict
- May become defensive and take innocuous comments personally
- May have difficulty juggling more than one or two complex ideas at a time

- May fail to see the effect on the future of actions taken in the present
- May not bother to adequately prepare

## APPLY IT

Your innate negotiation strengths and blind spots help and hurt you in negotiations. When negotiating, it's important to understand how your personal style can impact negotiations. For example, one of the authors of this book is an ENTP. Her strengths are that she is a creative problem solver, extremely perceptive, quick and flexible (she *is* a cheetah), charming and charismatic, and a quick study. However, she usually prefers to wing it and doesn't listen well (or she is not very interested in details). She is also relatively unrealistic (but doesn't see herself this way) and seems to change her mind frequently. Table 1.1 shows how her innate personality type has helped and hurt her in negotiating with different groups in her day-to-day work life.

In your notebook, create a table similar to table 1.1. Look at the groups of people you work with on a day-to-day basis and identify how your own personality style has helped and hurt you in the course of those interactions.

## REFLECT

When you are done, review the example and see how your work compares. Were you able to identify specific groups of people with whom you interact? In your notebook, give a short summary (in three words or less) of your perceptions of the work you did for this chapter. You will remember more about what you did if you can attach a succinct message with some emotion to what you just experienced.

Identify three things you learned by evaluating your personality type and the impact it has on your negotiation strengths and blind spots.

**Table 1.1** How the Author's ENTP Personality
Type Has Affected Relations with Different Groups

| Group | Helped | Hurt |
|-------|--------|------|
| Team Members | Motivates people to meet deadlines. Affectionately known as the butt kicker. | People have to put up a wind sock daily to see which direction they're going for the day. |
| Supervisors | Most have gone on to get other jobs (that were better) after they had her on their staff. | Well this is the reason she is an entrepreneur — she defines the term Alpha. She has to make it as an entrepreneur because most supervisor-style relationships just don't work for her. |
| Vendors | They benefit from her sea of ideas and how they can serve the growing needs of whatever project she gets going. | They tend to have a hard time delivering if they commit too soon before they fully understand what they are committing to. Also, most agree to her request for unrealistic deadlines and fail to deliver. |
| Customers | They benefit from products creatively adapted to their changing needs. | Her customers at times have a difficult time grasping how they can best use her company's products because she can offer a bewildering array of options. |

## Examples from Our Students

### Reflect — What Did I Learn?
- It is easier to focus on your blind spots when you know them.
- The self-discovery assessment was on target (scary).

- I have learned that my personality is evolving and changes over time.
- My career choice is good given my personality type, but there are weaknesses I really need to be aware of and pay heed to.

## ACT

Identify three things you're going to do differently in your next negotiation based on what you learned by understanding your personal negotiating strengths.

Since learning is a lifelong pursuit, identify three skills you want to improve because of what you learned in this chapter.

### Examples from Our Students

#### Act — What Will I Do Differently?
- Modify my own behaviors to be more of a team player.
- Think about my personality type as I interact with others on a daily basis.
- Be firmer in position instead of accommodating others needs — I will accommodate mine.
- Work on my listening skills.
- Improve my overall communication skills.
- Increase patience in making any decisions. Think more.
- Improve my social skills for developing rapport with people.

You've finished the first step of the Cheetah Negotiations process, understanding yourself. Negotiations can be a fulfilling experience when you negotiate in a way that best leverages your personal negotiation strengths. If you start to feel overwhelmed with the prospects of a negotiation, revisit this chapter and reacquaint yourself with your innate negotiation strengths. The next chapter builds on what you've learned in this chapter to understand other people's personalities, how it will impact their negotiating style, and how you can use this information to speed a negotiation so you can both get what you want, fast.

*Communication is not easy*
*Things can come out sounding cheesy*
*If you know their type*
*You can cut out all the hype*
*And talk without sounding sleazy*

# Who Are the Other Characters?

*I*n this chapter you will learn how to assess other people's personality types. The better you know the negotiating characteristics of other people, the better you can interact with them in a negotiation. The purpose of this knowledge is to interact with people using both sides' strengths, not to manipulate or take advantage of people. Considering that many negotiations are conducted with salespeople who are well versed in these techniques, it is imperative that you know this material as well to interact with them at the same level.

Some people can grasp other people's personalities quickly. (This is called speed-reading their personality type.) While this can be learned, it is also an innate talent. If you do not have the speed-reading talent, you might want to get someone on your team who does, especially when you are in the middle of important negotiations.

The goal here is to make you familiar with speed-reading as a specific tool. If you'd like to learn more about this topic, we recommend you purchase the book, *The Art of Speed Reading People: How to Size People Up and Speak Their Language.*

There are three steps here to learning how to best interact with people during negotiations. You have to take some time to understand their personality and how to best communicate with people of their personality type. Various professions attract people of similar personality types. When you are preparing for a negotiation, take some time to get to know the type of people with whom you will be negotiating. The next step is to understand how to best communicate with various personality types so you can clearly understand their requirements and best communicate your needs. The last step is to practice so that this becomes second nature. When you take the time to understand other people and how to communicate with them, it shows you have their interests in mind.

## STEP 1: KNOW THE CAST OF CHARACTERS

People with specific personality types are naturally attracted to the positions and careers that fit their type. For example, entrepreneurs are typically ENTP personality types. Where most people see a headache, the ENTP types see possibilities. They are open, optimistic, and full of enthusiasm for their ideas.

Consider an example. Let's say that you are purchasing a software system for your company. In your early negotiations, you deal directly with the owner of the company. If the owner started the company with a concept that he or she created, then this person is most likely an ENTP. If you were meeting with the owner, you'd use a different negotiating strategy than if you were meeting with a technician in that same company. The technician would most likely be more conservative than the owner — perhaps he or she has been working in the same industry for the past twenty years. In this case, the technician would probably be a personality type of

ISTJ. This person is probably very detail-oriented, wants to know the value here and now, and then wants to move on. He or she most likely doesn't want to spend hours exploring possibilities, like the owner/entrepreneur. This personality type just wants the facts and wants to know how he or she is going to make things work.

## Popular Occupation and Type

- **ENFJ:** Recruiter, Fund-raiser, Facilitator, Psychologist, Clergy/Ministry, Personal Counselor, Politician

- **INFJ:** Career Counselor, Psychologist, Priest/Clergy/Monk/Nun, Designer, Employee Assistance Program Coordinator/Counselor

- **ENFP:** Reporter, Marketing Consultant, Social Worker, Pastoral Counselor, Legal Mediator, Psychologist

- **INFP:** Architect, Editor, Legal Mediator, Counselor, Church Worker, Team Building/Conflict Resolution Consultant

- **ENTJ:** Credit Investigator, Stockbroker, Labor Relations, Attorney, Judge, Psychologist, Psychiatrist, Personnel Manager, Office Manager

- **INTJ:** Financial Planner, Computer Systems Analyst, Attorney: Administrative/Litigator, Designer

- **ENTP:** Politician, Financial Planner, Investment Banker, Entrepreneur, Inventor, Venture Capitalist

- **INTP:** Pharmacist, Lawyer, Psychologist/Psychoanalyst, Investigator, Legal Mediator, Psychiatrist

- **ESTJ:** Sales (tangibles): Computers/Real Estate, Security Guard, Police/Probation/Corrections Officer, Auditor, General Contractor, Loan Officer, Project Manager, Paralegal

- **ISTJ:** Auditor, Office Manager, Police Officer/Detective, Real Estate Agent, Corrections Officer, Bank Examiner, Electrician

- **ESFJ:** Counselor, Paralegal, Social Worker, Sales Representative, Retail Owner/Operator, Credit Counselor, Telemarketer

- **ISFJ:** Family Physician, Guidance Counselor, Probation Officer, Paralegal, Interior Decorator, Real Estate Agent/Broker

- **ESTP:** Police Officer, Real Estate Agent, Banker, Investor, Carpenter, General Contractor, Car Sales, Retail sales

- **ISTP:** Automotive Products Retailer, Police/Corrections Officer, Purchasing Agent, Carpenter, Banker, Paralegal

- **ESFP:** Police/Corrections Officer, Retail Sales/Management, Real Estate Agent, Primary Care Physician, Social Worker

- **ISFP:** Paralegal, Storekeeper, Social Worker, Police/Corrections Officer, Sports Equipment Sales, Primary Care Physician

When you are negotiating, try to do some homework and find out the type of position your counterpart holds. The more information you can get about the position of the people around the table, the better you can prepare your negotiation strategy.

Chapter 1 provided a summary of the negotiating strengths and weaknesses of the various personality types. Table 2.1 lists the dominant personality characteristic for each personality type.

*Table 2.1* Each Personality Type's Dominant Personality Characteristic

| Dominant Trait | Personality Types | | | |
|---|---|---|---|---|
| Intuitive | ENTP | ENFP | INTJ | INFJ |
| Sensory | ESTP | ESFP | ISTJ | ISFJ |
| Thinkers | ENTJ | ESTJ | INTP | ISTP |
| Feelers | ESFJ | ENFJ | INFP | ISFP |

When you're evaluating your counterparts in a negotiation, find out their chosen career, and not necessarily the position they currently hold. Their chosen career can give you clues about their personality type, so once you know this you can take a guess at their personality type. For example, we were negotiating with a supplier who started out his career as an attorney. From what we know about people attracted to a profession as a lawyer, he was most likely an INTJ personality. This means that his dominant personality characteristic is intuitive and he may be more attracted to discussing ideas rather than facts and data.

### Tips for Reading People's Personality Types

To read someone's personality, notice their behavior around others. E or I — Extrovert (E) or Introvert (I) — relates to how people are energized. Do they get excited and animated around others (E)? Or do they prefer to be off on their own (I)?

To read someone's personality, notice where they place their focus. N or S — Intuitive (N) or Sensory (S) — relates to what people focus on in their environment. Do they look at "what could be" (N)? Or do they see "what is" (S)? People who fit the "N" classification are "idea" people and the people who fit the "S" classification are driven by "real" facts and data.

To read someone's personality notice how they make decisions. T or F — Thinker (T) or Feeler (F) — relates to how people make decisions. Do they make decisions impersonally, prefacing comments with "I think..." (T)? Or do they make decisions based on their own values, sometimes prefacing comments with "I feel..." (F)?

To read someone's personality, notice the state of their desk. J or P — Judging (J) or Perceiving (P) — relates to how people choose to live. Do they prefer to keep their desk neat and tidy (i.e., very structured) (J)? Or do they prefer to keep it more spontaneously organized (i.e., very flexible) (P)? People who fit the "J" classification prefer an orderly life and are happiest when matters are settled. People who fit the "P" classification prefer to be spontaneous and are happiest when their lives are more flexible.

## The Relationship Factor

In day-to-day life we negotiate with people in a wide range of relationships. Team members are peer-to-peer relationships. Supervisors have some power over us to decide our work assignments and compensation. Customers are people who purchase our products or services. Sales representatives are people who are selling products or services. People who work as team members, supervisors, customers, or vendors can have any of the personality types. Their career is more of an indicator of their personality style than their relationship to you.

The reason we highlight the relationship is that it impacts the power position in the negotiation. You would naturally negotiate differently with a team member than with a supervisor, and you would treat a customer (someone who was purchasing something from you) differently than a sales rep (someone who you were purchasing something from). For these examples we are just looking at professional relationships. But you can do the same thing for personal relationships — relationships with parents, children, siblings, spouse, and friends.

**_Table 2.2_ Identifying Personality Type by a Chosen Career**

| Relationship | Name | Career | Indicators | Personality Type |
|---|---|---|---|---|
| Team Member | Andre | Teacher | Reads magazines at parties, dreamer, thinks things through, organized | INTJ |
| Supervisor | Bob | COO | Doesn't like to be bothered, wants to know impact on the bottom line and how it fits with strategic direction; always impeccably dressed, a scientist | ISTJ |
| Sales Representative | Andrew | Advertising Account Representative | Always on the go, full of ideas, very emotional, and rather scattered | ENFP |
| Customer | Mary | Project Manager | Detail oriented, wants a proven solution, thinks things through in a logical progression, very organized, likes to be in charge | ESTJ |

All involve a different approach to negotiating depending on the nature of the relationship.

## STEP 2: IDENTIFY COMMUNICATION TACTICS

In the personality type indicators, there are four basic communication styles: NT, NF, SJ, and SP. The way someone chooses to communicate with you tells you much about their personality. It also tells you a lot about how you can best communicate with them in a negotiation.

## NT — Conceptualizers

They see possibilities and analyze them to logically pursue the opportunities. They have vision, are great innovators, and build systems to achieve their goals. However, they can get too complex for others to understand, overlook necessary details, and have trouble with authority and rules.

## NF — Idealists

They can bring out the best in others, are excellent at resolving conflict, and are good motivators. They are good communicators. However, they tend to make decisions based on their own opinions and at the same time have trouble being detached from others' problems.

## SJ — Traditionalists

They pay attention to regulations and timelines, and they pride themselves in doing the right thing in every situation, every time. However, they tend to exist very much in the "here and now" and are not into long-range planning.

## SP — Experiencers

They are resourceful at attacking immediate problems and do well in very loose structures. However, they can be unpredictable, don't fully think through the ramifications of their actions, and tend to lose enthusiasm once the crisis situation of a problem is over.

## STEP 3: PRACTICE, PRACTICE, PRACTICE

In the previous step, we looked at people you interact with on a routine basis to help develop speed-reading skills. However, in many negotiations you have to think fast on your feet and may

**Table 2.3** Identifying Communication Tactics

| Relationship | Name | Personality Type | Communication Style | Communication Tactics |
|---|---|---|---|---|
| Team Member | Andre | INTJ | Short phone calls, likes to show what he's done, wants acknowledgement, and he finds the good in other people. | Be brief and to the point, take time to look at his work; and thank him — especially in front of others. |
| Supervisor | Bob | ISTJ | Doesn't want to be bothered with details — just wants a solution, a price, and know how it's going to make him look. | Make sure to know his current challenges and find a solution that will solve his immediate problem. |
| Sales Representative | Andrew | ENTP | Wants to share ideas, enroll you in participating, and usually needs funding for some grandiose scheme — and needs your project to fund it. | Agree to participate in a small part of his latest brainstorm. Also, be very clear about the deliverable and how he will be paid. Hold off paying most of the money until the final product is delivered. |
| Customer | Mary | ESTJ | Very busy for anything but a short catch up most of the time. Will talk extensively though about her sports training, and likes to help people and solve problems. | Schedule an appointment to talk with her and engage her in a discussion. Ask about her family and sports training. Ask about the ways she can help in the situation or problem. |

## *Table 2.4* Analyzing Characters' Personality Types

| Character | Type | Indicators |
|---|---|---|
| Gilligan | ENFP | He is lazy when no one else is around but gets energized and animated when other people are around (E). He tends to have half-baked ideas and doesn't think things through (N) and is fairly irrational and emotional (F). He is also somewhat wishy-washy and messy (P). |
| The Skipper | ISTJ | He prefers solitude (I), gets caught up in the details (S), is very logical (T), and likes to keep things organized and live by rules (J). |
| The Professor | INTJ | He is energized in doing research when he is alone (I). Is into far out ideas (N). He is very analytical and doesn't notice much how people around him feel (T) and he is very methodical in the way he carries out his experiments (J). |
| Maryanne | ISFP | She is shy and prefers to be alone (I). She seems consumed with daily chores (S). She spends a lot of time focusing on her own and other peoples' feelings (F). At times she appears scatterbrained and prefers to leave her options open (P). |
| Ginger | ENTJ | She is gregarious and outgoing (E). She dreams up schemes to get people to do what it is she wants them to do (N). She tends to be very logical in how she pursues what it is she wants and doesn't pay much attention to other people's feelings (T). She is very methodical about how she goes after what she wants and pays close attention to how she presents herself (J). |
| Mr. Howell | INTP | He is really into himself and his own interests (I). He thinks in big idea terms (N) and makes decisions from logical thought processes (T). He prefers to continuously explore options and thinks that rules don't apply to him (P). |
| Mrs. Howell (Lovey) | ESFJ | She loves to throw parties (E). She is very focused on day-to-day details and doesn't want to be bothered with all that other "nonsense" (S). She gets easily flustered and operates day-to-day by how she is feeling (F). She likes to keep things very orderly and tidy and expects others to do the same (J). |

not have the luxury of taking the time to analyze your counter-parts' personality. To develop your skills with speed-reading people, analyze characters from the sitcoms, movies, or books with which you are most familiar.

The authors watched way too much TV as kids and in table 2.4 are the characters from one of their favorite sitcoms, *Gilligan's Island*.

## APPLY IT

### Activity 1
Identify people in each of the categories listed in table 2.2 with whom you've interacted. They can be people from the past and present, or people you anticipate interacting with in the future. Identify their chosen career, which is not necessarily the position they currently hold. Chosen career can give you clues about personality type, so once you know this you can take a guess at their personality type. Record your results in your notebook.

### Activity 2
In your notebook, reproduce table 2.2 and see if you can determine the personality types of some of the people you work with.

### Activity 3
Assess how each person in the table you've created has communicated with you in the past. Identify the best way for you to communicate with them (see table 2.3 for an example). Record your results in your notebook.

### Activity 4
Take a stab at identifying the personality types of characters from your favorite TV shows, movies, and books. Identify the indicators that led you to make that assessment. Record the results in your notebook.

**REFLECT**

Review our examples in this chapter and see how your work compares. What was the most challenging part of these exercises for you? Give a short summary (in three words or less) of your perceptions of the work you did for this chapter. You will remember more about what you did if you can attach a succinct message with some emotion to what you just experienced.

Identify three things you learned in this chapter.

## Examples from Our Students

### Reflect — What Did I Learn?

- I cannot speed-read people. This took me way too long to complete!
- Knowing team members' personality types and communication preferences will make me more productive in future negotiations.
- I learned that people have different personalities by the way that they process information and get energy.
- It is critical to develop relationships with other participants and to learn to understand them.
- I learned more about the personality types of others and how they see things compared to how I see them.

 **ACT**

Identify three things you're going to do differently in your next negotiation by understanding other people's personality type.

Since learning is a lifelong pursuit, identify three skills you want to improve because of what you learned in this chapter.

## Examples from Our Students

### Act — What Will I Do Differently?

- Gauge other people's personality types before I get into negotiations.
- Be friendlier with the people involved, develop rapport.
- Do my homework to figure out the opponent's personality types.
- Won't deal with different personality types in the same manner.
- As my personality evolves, I must remember that others' personalities are also changing.
- Think before I speak. Be careful to communicate the way someone prefers instead of what I am comfortable with.
- Improve on my social skills for developing rapport with people.
- I will try to value people with different personalities and utilize or complement their strengths.

You can leverage other people's personality strengths to help them get what they want fast so you can get what you want fast. By doing this and negotiating with them in a way that works well for them as well as for you, you will be validating who they are as a human being and you will have fantastic results. This is the art of a Cheetah Negotiator.

*Section Two*
# Setting the Stage

Negotiations are a dance on the stage of life. There are those who get out onto the dance floor looking like total klutzes, and then there are those who get out there and gracefully move through the scene. The information and examples in this section are designed to enable you to set the stage for quick and effective negotiations for all the situations you encounter. You'll be able to set the stage of your negotiations so that you can get out on the negotiation dance floor like a pro.

BATNA ZOPA & GUAL
Three things to remember for all
You can never lose
With the options to choose
From BATNA, ZOPA, and GUAL

# Chapter Three

# What Do You Want? What Do They Want?

*I*n this chapter you will learn how to clarify what you want in a negotiation. You're also going to identify clues that tell you what the other party wants. This process has two parts:

1. Determine what you want by identifying your objectives and priorities.
2. Determine the importance of your relationship with the other party involved and the importance of the outcome of the negotiation.

Setting the stage enables all parties to quickly and effectively achieve their objectives. Being prepared also helps make the best use of people's time. To best prepare we have outlined several simple steps:

- Establish context.
- Identify needs and wants.
- Understand what will happen if you don't reach an agreement.

- Establish the importance of the negotiation outcome.
- Understand the importance of the relationship with the other party.
- Determine the zone of possible agreement (ZOPA).
- Be clear on where you won't compromise and when you will get up and leave (GUAL) a negotiation.

## NEGOTIATION OBJECTIVES

The first job in setting the stage for a negotiation is understanding want you want to come away with. The very fact that you are negotiating indicates that you are interested in coming to a consensus with another party for something you want or need. Therefore, you must clarify what you're going after and why. "Beware lest you lose the substance by grasping at the shadow" (Bartlett's, 60).

Determine what is truly important to the outcome of the negotiation. This enables you to be more focused on objectives and less ego-directed. Some people negotiate based on their "position" — that is, what they think should happen. However, what is "right" is based on the best possible outcome for both parties. Getting locked into a position based on what you think is right will slow down and derail a negotiation.

### Positions vs. Objectives

The basic premise for understanding the difference between positions and objectives is that positions tend to be driven by emotion (most often a negative and harmful emotion), whereas objectives are driven more by principle (more often associated with a positive outcome).

You need to clarify the difference between your needs and your wants. *Needs* means the item is necessary for success. *Wants* represent improvements of some sort. You also need to understand the "why" of this negotiation. To understand the "why,"

**_Table 3.1_ Examples of Positions vs. Objectives in Adversarial Situations**

| Adversarial Situation | Position | Objective |
|---|---|---|
| Divorce | Make him/her PAY for mistakes | Create the best life possible for the children |
| Competitor lawsuit | Punish them for perceptions of "wrong doing" | Protect my company |
| Estate settlement | Get my fair share | Disperse assets among heirs |
| Property line disputes | I am right | Find out the property line with a legal survey |
| Adolescents wanting more freedom | I'm the parent so you have to listen to me | Provide age-appropriate freedoms for which the children are mature enough to handle problems they encounter |
| Cut off in traffic | You moron – I'm going to get you back | Get to the desired destination |
| Purchased a product that didn't work | Don't get ripped off | Get a product that works |
| Prosecuting a criminal | Make him suffer for committing the crime | Prevent the criminal from repeating the offense and provide possible restitution for the victim |

you have to determine what would happen if nothing comes out of your negotiation. In the book *Getting to Yes: Negotiating Agreement Without Giving In* by Fisher and Ury, this is referred to as your "Best Alternative to a Negotiated Agreement," or BATNA. Generating a BATNA will help you develop ideas for the next steps to take if your negotiation goes south. Just by the act of making this consideration, you may come up with other creative solutions to your issue.

## RELATIONSHIP VS. OUTCOME — PRIORITIES

All negotiations are not equal. There are two value elements to every negotiation and it is important to understand the values of each specific negotiation.

The first value element is the importance of the relationship, and not all relationships are equally important. Your methods of communication and compromise will vary widely based on how important the long-term relationship with the other party is to you. For example, a team member with whom you will be working with continuously over a two-to-three year period will get different consideration than a one-time interaction you have with a salesperson. Another thing to keep in mind regarding relationships is "what you do not want done to yourself, do not do to others" (Bartlett's, 63).

The second element to consider is the relative importance of your outcome. You may be able to be very flexible in some situations and the outcome may not be as important as other situations. For example, if you are shopping for a generic ink jet printer, you can be fairly detached from the outcome of the price of any one model because there are so many to choose from. However, if there is only one company that supplies a critical software package you need for the success of your project, you have much less leverage on price. Once you understand these two elements for any negotiation, you can plot them on the outcome vs. relationship matrix.

## KNOW YOUR ZOPA AND GUAL

ZOPA — stands for the zone of possible agreement. This is the zone in which you are in agreement. You may be able to estimate this prior to a negotiation. During the introduction stage of the actual negotiation you may get further clarity on this zone.

GUAL — stands for get up and leave. What happens when you go into a negotiation in good faith but the other party has other

**Figure 3.1** Relationship vs. Outcome Matrix

| | | Low | High |
|---|---|---|---|
| Relationship | High | Team member negotiations for sharing routine project tasks | Purchasing a one-of-a-kind software solution that needs ongoing support |
| | Low | Purchasing an ink jet printer | Purchasing a car or a house |
| | | Low | High |
| | | Outcome | |

intentions, is dishonest, or proposes something so outrageous that it offends you? You have the choice to get up and leave (GUAL). You should understand what you and your team's GUAL issues are prior to going into a negotiation. You can end the negotiation by simply saying, "This isn't the right situation for us right now. Let me go back and think about it and get back in touch with you later. Thank you for your time."

There are two common situations that would precipitate a GUAL response. The first one is when the other party makes or counters offers that are multiples away from your concept of what constitutes a reasonable offer. This typically means either you or they have not done adequate research on the aspects under proposal driving the price. The second area is when the other party makes suggestions that are illegal or unethical or you perceive that the other party is being dishonest. There are enough other ways in this world to achieve your objectives that you do not need to compromise your values to continue a negotiation with a dishonest and unethical person. Nor do you need to chastise the other person — they may just see the situation differently than you do. The best course of action is to be polite and to leave.

Figure 3.2 shows the GUAL and the ZOPA for a negotiation with an employee for a pay raise. It shows the employer's and the employee's needs and wants. It identifies where they currently

*Figure 3.2* GUAL – ZOPA Range

| GUAL — 33% above market value | ZOPA — Vacation, benefits, job deliverables, performance | GUAL — 25% below market value |
|---|---|---|
| **Employer** — Needs to pay people what they can afford for the value they deliver. Needs to keep qualified, productive people on staff. Wants to maximize productivity. | measurements, match of company needs to employees' interests, skills and aspirations, and quality of life with the job. Pay has to be at the high range of industry standard compensation to attract and keep highly qualified and productive staff. | **Employee** — Needs to support self and family. Wants to be paid for the value they deliver to the business. |

have agreement (ZOPA) and their respective boundaries where they will negotiate (GUAL).

## PRIORITIES AND OBJECTIVES — AN EXAMPLE

Here is an example of identifying objectives with BATNA, priorities with the relationships and outcomes assessment, the ZOPA, and the GUAL. Use table 3.2 to first analyze both parties' objectives and priorities, then identify the ZOPA and your GUAL.

### Context

You work for Cheetah Coding and you're on a fast-track software development project for the town's public works website. The website has to get community input for the new sewage treatment plant. You have less than a month to get something up, or things could get stinky.

### Negotiation

You need to negotiate with another functional manager for more resources for your project.

**Table 3.2** Objectives and Priorities Table for YOU

| My Situation | Needs/ Wants | Why | BATNA | Relationship | Outcome |
|---|---|---|---|---|---|
| We are on a fast-track software development project | Needs: Additional Java programmers<br><br>Wants: In-house resources from the software department. Specifically we want Bob because of his Java experience. | Less expensive to the project because of the way the project is charged for the in-house programmer's time. Also, we know the person we want and the skills we need. | We could put out an RFQ on the Java programmers resource website. | Low: We're willing to go outside for help. | High: We need the programming. |

## Personality

Phil Dhup (an ISTJ) is the functional manager for the software department. He wants details — lots of them. Phil spends his day sitting behind his closed office door because he's a closet coder himself. He isn't the most communicative person on the planet and guards his programming resources for his pet projects zealously. The sewage treatment website is not glamorous and is not one of his pet projects.

Table 3.2 documents your objectives and priorities.

## ZOPA

We both want a well-managed project that makes the best use of scarce resources.

*Table 3.3* Objectives and Priorities for THEM

| Their Situation | Needs/ Wants | Why | BATNA | Relationship | Outcome |
|---|---|---|---|---|---|
| The software department has a high demand for Bob because he is a very good Java programmer. | Needs: To best manage Bob's time between multiple projects<br><br>Wants: To make sure that the project is well managed so that Bob doesn't waste his time. | If the project manager tells Bob's boss he only needs Bob for 30 hours, and it is really an 80-hour job, then it makes it very difficult for him to have Bob adequately support the other projects. | Develop a preferred supplier list of qualified contracting support. | Low: We have a lot of projects to support. | Low: There is more work than we can handle. |

## GUAL

If we are asked to do any unethical or illegal favors in exchange for getting Bob's time, we will get up and leave.

In this example, we demonstrated an appreciation for the manager's position. We can proceed by examining all the alternatives: priorities, in-house vs. outsourced manpower, additional schedule with overtime, options, and so forth.

## APPLY IT

Now that we have shown you an example, we offer four scenarios so you can get some practice. Create the objective and priority

matrices for each scenario in your notebook. Identify the anticipated ZOPA and your GUAL for each scenario.

Create tables like tables 3.2 and 3.3 for YOU and for THEM for
the following four scenarios.

## Scenario 1

### Context

A contractor has done work for you in the past and hasn't per-
formed to expectation. He does, however, have materials in his
possession that he has created for you and not quite delivered. You
would like these materials, and, in addition, you have a project
that could take advantage of the work he's already done.

### Negotiation

You want to negotiate for the project and get value for the money
you have already spent.

### Personality

Anton, an ENTP, generates tons of great ideas; one problem is his
follow-through. He talks nonstop and paints a picture that leaves
you breathless with the possibilities. The other problem is performance; you have difficulty getting a picture of his work break-
down structure or schedule.

## Scenario 2

### Context

Your company sells point-of-sale systems, Cheetah Cash, to busi-
nesses in your community. Your experience shows that while the
software is what you might call inexpensive or cheap, the true
value of entertaining a new client is the long-term maintenance
contract that results from the sale of the software.

### Negotiation

You have scheduled a meeting with a new restaurant, Cheetah Chews, which is opening in the area.

### Personality

You met the owner of this franchise, Lucy (an INFJ), at a chamber of commerce function where you found her reading a magazine in the corner. You struck up a short conversation with her and learned about her new restaurant opening. While the conversation was short, you can tell she is excited about Cheetah Chews. The cheetah is her favorite animal, and she keeps a picture of one in a locket around her neck. She has been planning for this restaurant for two years and you can tell she's done all her homework and is working according to an exact schedule.

## Scenario 3

### Context

Randy, one of your team members, is proving to be both brilliant and troublesome at the same time. Your current project is in the execution stage, and he is a major contributor to the software programming that is required for Cheetah Cloning. However, the stress of the tight schedule and demands have set him on edge and he occasionally blows his top at the worst possible moment; the last time was in the middle of a sponsor presentation on the status of the project. After each blowup, he generally retreats to his office and is unavailable to communicate with people for two days.

### Negotiation

Randy blew up yesterday and you need him to test and debug the last software routine written by more junior staff by tomorrow.

### Personality

Needless to say, Randy (an ISTP) presents a brilliant but moody individual. He doesn't usually contribute at meetings, if he shows up at all. His office looks like a cyclone hit it, but he can find anything he needs instantly. He is a maestro of software, far more comfortable in front of a computer screen than another face. His expertise comes across as blunt criticism to new ideas; the logic in his brain loses any tact by the time it leaves his mouth. However, he is very punctual with his work and is most comfortable being in control of his situation.

## Scenario 4

### Context

You are dealing with the project sponsor for a quality improvement project. The team is at a point where they have researched and selected a software solution for capturing quality control data. After a rather slow start, the team, which is cross-functional from various departments of the manufacturing company Cheetah Chairs, is finally performing to your satisfaction and progressing well.

### Negotiation

You and the team are meeting with the sponsor, Dewey Waite, to get approval for the purchase of your quality control software.

### Personality

Dewey (an ESFP) is a founder at Cheetah Chairs and has three months until retirement. While this is a pet project of his, the rest of the company has been slow to pick up the quality banner. Dewey has no real job at this point; he spends his time cornering unsuspecting employees and spending large amounts of time relating stories about the good old days. He has adopted your team as his new watering hole, which is the reason the team got off to a slow start. Now he wants to go over all the research that went into looking at SPC software in excruciating detail. He feels very passionate about the company and feels the quality project will help protect his legacy. At the same time he seems to be putting off the decision on the software purchase by asking for more and more analysis. Half of the time he is very late to your meetings, and has left most of the items he needs back in his office, returns to your meeting unable to have found what he needed anyway.

 **REFLECT**

When you are done, review our examples and see how your work compares. What was the most challenging part of this exercise for you? Give a short summary (in three words or less) of your perceptions of the work you did for this chapter. You will remember more about what you did if you can attach a succinct message with some emotion to what you just experienced.

Identify three things you learned by identifying each party's objectives and priorities.

### Examples from Our Students

#### Reflect– What Did I Learn?

- Looking at the other side's perspective makes me clearer on what I really want.
- Considering what is really important to me and the other viewpoints I will be interacting with is very valuable going in.
- The most helpful thing is identifying what you want to negotiate. The exercise for my situation and their situation, needs, and so forth, helps to identify common ground. It is helpful to know what each party already agrees on.

## ACT

Identify three things you're going to do differently in your next negotiation by understanding how to identify each party's objectives and priorities.

Since learning is a lifelong pursuit, identify three skills you want to improve because of what you learned in this section.

## Examples from Our Students

### Act — What Will I Do Differently?

- Be more aware of what I need to do to satisfy the needs and wants of other participants in the negotiation while at the same time reaching my own objectives.
- Seek to understand all of the participants more deeply.
- Become less frustrated by people who can't justify what they want (their requirements).
- Identify what the people I am negotiating with want.
- Understand what I need.
- Understand the participation matrix and their needs and wants and where everyone can benefit.

Negotiating is a daily activity that can be an exhilarating challenge rather than a destructive conflict resulting from each side's adversarial positioning. The main source of conflict is differing expectations. Many times people don't even fully grasp their own expectations. With the concepts and activities presented in this chapter, you can better understand your own and others' expectations. This reduces those conflicts that are so common in negotiations. Along with that firm grasp on expectations, you must also evaluate the importance of the relationship with the other party. With this knowledge, you can work toward getting what you want, fast. In the next chapter you learn how to set up the physical space so negotiations proceed at Cheetah speed.

Sometimes when things get tense
You need tools to help you make sense
You can breathe, you can stretch,
There's water to fetch
To help from going over the fence

# Chapter Four

# Creating the Backdrop

*I*n this chapter, you will create the backdrop for the negotiation. Armed with the understanding of what both you and your counterpart want, you can ask yourself who you want to be for this negotiation. You can learn to emotionally detach yourself from the situation so that you can be successful with many types of temperaments.

In the previous chapter, you made some discoveries about personalities. It may be that you have difficulty being flexible in your role. Being conscious of your role and the way you are perceived, being likeable, asking permission, and other techniques are useful tools to have at your disposal when the time comes for negotiations. Now you will look at setting the stage with the external environment. Depending on the negotiation, you can augment the atmosphere by serving the right food, having great creative "tools" available to help look at solutions in a different light, and even making use of music. These techniques can help bring minds to a collaborative solution.

Negotiation situations can be stressful for many people. For quick and effective negotiations, it's best if all parties stay calm and relaxed. This can be difficult in a stressful and contentious situation. There are a number of techniques you can use to keep yourself calm and to set up the environment so the other parties stay calm and relaxed as well.

In some situations you need to play hardball, while in other situations you need to team with another person to play good cop, bad cop. Sometimes you must be the reconciler and mediator. Based on your innate personality, you'll be stronger in some roles than in others. For critical negotiations that require a role outside of your comfort zone, you need to enlist other people on your negotiation team to fulfill those roles.

There are critical components to create the backdrop for successful negotiations:

- Consciously choose your demeanor so you can be successful in even the most heated negotiation.
- Identify roles for different negotiation situations, and know when it's valuable to involve other people who are more innately qualified for the different negotiation situations than you may be yourself.
- Create the environment so you can better generate specific negotiation outcomes.

We recommend a three-step process to set the stage for a successful negotiation:

1. Emotionally and physically prepare yourself for the negotiation.
2. Evaluate your roles and strengths in the negotiation.
3. Prepare the meeting environment.

## STEP 1: EMOTIONALLY AND PHYSICALLY PREPARE YOURSELF FOR THE NEGOTIATION

Negotiation situations can be stressful. To be effective in a negotiation, you need to stay calm and relaxed. In a tense and contentious situation, this can be difficult. These recommendations help you to create the demeanor that will enable you to be successful in even the most heated negotiation. Playing these various roles requires you to maintain a deep level of emotional detachment. There are a number of techniques you can use to remain calm, cool, and detached in any situation. Being aware of who you need to be in a negotiation enables you to play the role you need to play to achieve success.

### Diet

Diet plays a large role in how you perceive and react to any situation. The food and drink you consume can help you to be more relaxed in the types of situations that make many people stressed. A high-protein diet that avoids caffeine can reduce the effects of stress and help you stay calm and levelheaded. Before a tense negotiation, make sure you avoid foods that are high in sugar and carbohydrates. If you are entering into a negotiation in the morning, skip the donuts and coffee. Instead, have eggs, cheese, or a fruit smoothie made from just fruit and tofu. If you are entering into a negotiation in the afternoon, have the chef salad for lunch and skip the soda and pizza or submarine sandwich. Vitamin B is known as the stress-busting vitamin. As adults age, they are more prone to developing vitamin B deficiencies. Vitamin B complex supplements may help, but check with your doctor prior to making any dietary changes including taking vitamins.

### Breathing Exercises

We all breathe — in and out, in and out, in and out. We're usually totally unaware of how we breathe because it's one of those subconscious functions that our bodies perform to survive. Paying attention to how you breathe, just for one or two minutes, is usually enough for most people to calm down and become more relaxed. In our accelerated exam-prep classes, every ninety minutes we have our students do a technique we call alternative nostril breathing. This helps them stay calm, relaxed, and focused. Prior to entering a negotiation session and during breaks, take a couple of minutes to pay attention to your breathing to get calm and refocused. Here's how to do it:

- Start by placing your finger on your right nostril to hold it shut.
- Breathe in deeply through the left nostril — deep into the diaphragm in your abdomen — not into your lungs. Breathe in for four counts. Hold the breath for four counts.
- Place your finger on your left nostril and hold it shut. Exhale to the count of four through your right nostril. Hold it for a count of four.
- Breathe in again for a count of four through the right nostril while holding the left nostril closed. Hold it for a count of four.
- Exhale through the left nostril for a count of four. Hold it for a count of four.
- Start again by holding the right nostril shut.
- Repeat this whole cycle ten times.

### Physical Exercise

Exercise also plays a large role in helping you to stay calm and reduce stress. Walking just fifteen minutes a day can help people stay more relaxed. We teach a series of stretches in our accelerated exam-prep class that help people stay calm and focused. We have people do them every ninety minutes in class and every hour while they are taking their exams. If you know you're going into a negotiation, factor in a fifteen-minute walk in the morning. Prior

*Figure 4.1* Stretches to Relax and Rejuvinate

| 1. Mountain Pose | 2. Rag Doll |
|---|---|
| • Sweep arms up over head<br>• Feet shoulder width apart<br>• Shoulder blades try to touch<br>• Slightly tilt head back<br>• Hold for 15 seconds | • Sweep your arms down and just hang near floor (this is not a touch your toes stretch). It's just a hang<br>• Hold for 15 seconds |
| 3. Right Lunge | 4. Plank |
| • Move hands forward on floor<br>• Move right leg into lunge (stay on floor)<br>• Left foot points forward and try to have heel on the ground<br>• Hold for 15 seconds | • Move your hands forward<br>• Move the right leg back<br>• Hold your body straight like a plank<br>• Hold for 5 seconds |
| 5. Cobra | 6. Left Lunge |
| • Drop from plank onto floor<br>• Put your hands under your shoulders and push your head and shoulders up<br>• Arch your back and keep your hips on the floor<br>• Hold for 15 seconds<br>• Drop to the floor<br>• Rise to knees, drop head on floor<br>• Hold for 15 seconds | • Move up into a rag doll<br>• Move left leg into lunge (stay on floor)<br>• Right foot points forward and try to have heel on the ground<br>• Hold for 15 seconds |
| 7. Rag Doll | 8. Mountain Pose |
| • Sweep your arms down and just hang near floor (this is not a touch your toes stretch); it's just a hang<br>• Hold for 15 seconds | • Sweep arms up over head<br>• Feet shoulder width apart<br>• Shoulder blades try to touch<br>• Slightly tilt head back<br>• Hold for 15 seconds |

to going into a tense negotiation, take three to five minutes to stretch. Figure 4.1 illustrates a series of stretches you can easily do to stay relaxed and calm.

### Laughing

Laughter is the number one stress reliever. While you're in the middle of a tense negotiation, laughing might not be the best solution; however, you can prepare yourself with a good chuckle. One of the techniques that has worked well for us is to keep a success journal of negotiation experiences. Make sure to record some funny things in there. Just prior to entering the negotiation, review your journal and have a good laugh.

### Rituals

You'll notice sports players performing their rituals during games — wearing a lucky arm band, bouncing the basketball three times before making a free throw, etcetera. You can develop your own rituals for staying calm. Hypnotists do this with their patients under hypnosis. This ritual can be as simple as going to get a drink of water prior to entering a stressful situation, or as complicated as selecting an outfit that gets you into a more relaxed and calm frame of mind. Whatever it is, if you think it makes you more relaxed and calm, it is not distracting to other people, and it is appropriate for the current situation, make sure you follow it when you're in situations that might get heated.

### Detached

The less you're attached to one specific outcome, the more emotionally detached you can be during a negotiation. You and the parties with whom you're negotiating just might come up with a better solution than what any of you may have been able to develop on your own. Awareness of being detached is the first step. If you have a problem detaching from a situation, visualize yourself being a fly on the wall during your encounter. If things get too heated for you and you find yourself unable to detach emotionally to a situation, it's okay to take a fifteen-minute break to do the stretching and breathing to get back in perspective.

In *Non-Violent Communication, A Language of Life: Create Your Life, Your Relationships, and Your World in Harmony with Your Values*, Marshall Rosenberg presents a way to remain detached in heated situations. By following these tips you can communicate in a way that will keep you detached. These tips can even help defuse tense situations. There are four components to his model:

1. **Observe rather than evaluate**. If you notice a participant looking at their watch, an observation response is, "I see you are looking at your watch." That is an observational response. An evaluation response is, "It looks like you're pressed for time."

2. **Express your feelings**. If you are feeling frustrated because you don't think the other side is listening to you, it would be more effective to say, "I feel frustrated when I speak and I see that you are reading e-mail on your BlackBerry pager," instead of saying, "You are not listening to me."

3. **Acknowledge needs and take responsibility for your feelings**. Building on the previous example you would say, "I feel frustrated when I speak and I see that you are reading e-mail on your BlackBerry pager because I need to know that you are paying attention to what I am saying."

4. **Express requests in terms of concrete actions**. For example, "I would like to go over this book chapter by chapter while we are together so that we can see how the book

flows from beginning to end. I will read the first chapter on the computer, pass the file to the next person who will read it on the computer, print it out, and then pass it to the next person."

A wonderful way to stay detached is to find the silver lining. If you can find the positive element of any situation, it makes it easier to stay calm, relaxed, and detached.

Try all of these tips over the next week and see how they work in helping you to stay calm and relaxed in tense situations. For example, if you drive home in rush hour traffic, do the breathing exercises when someone cuts you off (after you get your car back on the road) and see if it helps you to stay relaxed. If you have a tough meeting with a team member one morning, try going for a walk and eating a high-protein breakfast before going to work and see how you feel. Put yourself in situations that will push your emotional buttons and see if using some of these techniques helps you to stay calm, relaxed, and detached.

## STEP 2: YOUR ROLES AND STRENGTHS IN THE NEGOTIATION

There are six common roles played on a team during negotiations. In the numerous negotiation situations you encounter as a project manager, you may need to play several of these roles at different stages in the negotiation. And in the same negotiation, you'll go through five unique stages that also require different hats. We've coordinated the various negotiation roles with the classifications of de Bono's six "thinking hats."

 ### Leader — White Hat
Orchestrates the activities of the team and may organize the overall negotiation if it's on their turf. The leader attempts to be neutral and objective and focuses on facts and figures.

**_Table 4.1_ Stressors and Relaxation Technique Examples**

| Date | Stressors | Relaxation techniques | Outcome |
|------|-----------|----------------------|---------|
| 3/5/2003 | Contractor wanted an outrageous cancellation fee because we decided not to pursue a project. The contract had not been formally executed, but we had given a tentative approval to an informal proposal and were awaiting the formal contract. | Stretching, paying attention to breathing, and laughing (The cancellation terms were so outrageous they made us laugh.) | Contractor agreed to a reasonable cancellation fee based on actual expenses incurred. In exchange we received work done to date on our behalf. He parted with nasty words, so we will not be pursuing any other work with his firm. |
| 3/6/2003 | Two team members were arguing over who was going to get a new computer first, since one was on back order for two weeks. | Ate eggs for breakfast and went for a walk. | Had each team member write up the reasons why the other team member needed the computer first. They decided that the person with the most free time right now would get the new computer first since he had the time to set it up. |
| 3/7/2003 | Came home from work to find that the kids had left their snack wrappers and dirty dishes all over the TV room. | Did my count to ten ritual and breathing exercises. | Went and found the kids playing in the backyard. Gave them each a hug and told them how happy I was that it was the weekend and we could have fun together. They asked me if we could rent a movie and watch it together. We all cleaned the TV room together before we watched the movie. |

*(continued on p. 66)*

*Table 4.1* (continued from p. 65)

| Date | Stressors | Relaxation techniques | Outcome |
|------|-----------|----------------------|---------|
| 3/10/2003 | Had a phone conference planned for Monday morning with a client who let us know they were interviewing five other firms and was very free with telling us where they thought our deficiencies were. | Went on two long walks over the weekend. During the phone meeting I did breathing exercises. Decided to view their "input" as information that would help us to better position our product to meet their needs. | They thought I listened so well that they decided to set up an in-person meeting to see how we could work together. |
| 3/11/2003 | While upgrading a publishing program I needed for working with other people on my team for a quick turnaround project, the entire computer froze up. I had to call the help desk and was put on hold for fifteen minutes, then transferred between four different technicians for over an hour. | Prior to calling the help desk I did stretching and breathing. I also ate a mint because I use mints as a ritual to relax. | We got my computer up and running and while on hold, I had a chance to read the manual for the program so I have a much better idea of the new capabilities of this software and how I'll be able to use it more effectively and efficiently. |

### Good Cop — Yellow Hat

The good cop is very friendly. This team member asks questions that help the other parties clarify their positions and put them at ease. This role is overall sunny, positive, and very optimistic.

### Bad Cop — Black Hat

The bad cop is very argumentative and pokes holes in any proposal put forth by the other parties. Overall this role is somber and serious, cautious and careful. They are quick to point out the weaknesses in an idea.

### Hard Nosed — Red Hat

This team member is quick to anger and a hard-liner about the original negotiating position. This person gets emotional with a purpose. They place heavy emphasis on the value of their gut reactions and their intuition.

### Idea Person — Green Hat

This team member comes up with new ideas and ways of coming to agreement. They see an abundant set of possibilities and can often derail a negotiation with a confusing set of options and opportunities.

### Big Picture — Blue Hat

This person sees the high-level view and summarizes and coalesces many points. They are concerned with control and keeping the negotiation organized.

Table 4.2 displays six negotiation situations we've encountered in our jobs as project managers where we've had to use one of the six hats. We identified the hat and the reason for using the hat.

*Table 4.2* Negotiation Situation and Roles

| Negotiation Situation | Role/Hat & Reason | Skill Assessment |
|---|---|---|
| We have a vendor that has slipped the delivery date for a product three times already. | Hard Nose/Red Hat — They need to know how dissatisfied we are with their lackadaisical approach to the schedule. | Fair — I'm uncomfortable with confrontation and being tough. I think Matt would do a better job of being the heavy. |
| We have a manufacturing quality-improvement project team and need Wayne on the team because of his statistics background. He works for the engineering functional manager. | Good Cop/Yellow Hat — We need to point out all the benefits to his functional group because of the improvements in manufacturing, what Wayne will learn on this project, and the short time he'll be gone because he's more experienced. | Fair — I don't know Wayne's boss well and didn't feel that comfortable approaching him. Rudi would do a better sales job. |
| Our largest customer asked for expanded functionality of a customized software package. They want a cost estimate for doing this. | Leader/White Hat — They want facts and figures. | Excellent — I was able to put together a concise summary and they accepted it. |
| Our sales team recently held a brainstorming session on some new sales tactics. It's time to summarize and develop a plan to put them into action. | Big Picture/Blue Hat — The team needs a high-level view and to be organized so they can move forward. | Excellent — I did a fantastic job of wrapping it up and providing the final document. |

*(continued on p. 69)*

Then we assessed how skilled we were at that role in negotiation and who we could turn to for help in a similar situation.

*Table 4.2* (continued from page 68)

| Negotiation Situation | Role/Hat & Reason | Skill Assessment |
|---|---|---|
| We have a murder board to see if a project should continue. | Bad Cop/Black Hat — The team needs to have a complete look at all the flaws of the project. | Fair — I was uncomfortable making unfavorable comments about other people's work. Linda could do a much better job of this than I do. |
| The directors of the company need input for their opportunity scan to determine other markets for our products. | Idea Person/Green Hat — They need to know the possibilities of various ideas. | Good — My team and I were able to provide a number of market possibilities. I did a good job summarizing all of our input. |

## STEP 3: PREPARING THE MEETING ENVIRONMENT FOR THE NEGOTIATION

Now that you're ready for the negotiation, it's time to take a look at the meeting environment that will affect the negotiation. There are two important elements that have to be attended to for a negotiation meeting to be successful. The first deals with ensuring you are adequately prepared to discuss the topics of the negotiation. The second deals with ensuring that the meeting environment adequately fulfills people's basic needs so they can focus on the topic at hand.

Both of these elements are addressed by completing a negotiation meeting checklist. On this checklist is the basic information for the meeting — where, when, who, what, etcetera. It also includes information to assist in making sure the environment will meet the participants' basic needs. In many negotiations, you may not want to share this list with anyone else — it's your tool to ensure a quick and effective negotiation. Many of your negotiations may also be fast and impromptu affairs. If you use this list routinely, preparing the environment for a quick and effective negotiation will become habit. You won't have to use the list after a while for everyday negotiation situations. You'll naturally remember the elements for effective negotiations. It's a good idea though to rely on the checklist for more formal and very important negotiations.

Let's review the basic elements.

## Logistics

The first part of the form documents the basic logistical information for the meeting — location, date, and the start and stop time. It's best to limit most negotiation meetings to fewer than two hours. This will better focus people's attention and bring issues to closure faster. To make sure the meeting ends in less than two hours, schedule the end time close to lunch instead of at the end of the day. Also, make sure that you and others on your team have to be somewhere at lunchtime. If you schedule the meeting toward the end of the day, there is a tendency for one party to request that people stay late to continue dialogue. If the meeting is offsite, make sure you set the tone by making your time constraints known. One technique you can use if you have a group calendaring system is to block off a standing meeting on your calendar from 3:30 – 5:00. This will prevent people from scheduling meetings with you late in the day.

## Participation Matrix

Use this section to document who is participating, the reason for their participation, their contact information, and to note when they have confirmed participation. If you are sharing this with all the negotiating parties, you might want to have two versions of this form. There are times when you don't want the other party to know why certain people are participating.

## Food

Regardless of the length of the meeting, it's important to serve food. We don't recommend you serve coffee and donuts, but if they are made available, make sure the people on your negotiating team know to avoid these foods. Coffee is a known diuretic and causes excess anxiety. The sugar and carbohydrates in the donuts also increases anxiety and will cause drowsiness. It's best to serve fruit, vegetables, cheese, nuts, water, and decaffeinated coffee and tea. Prior to the negotiating meeting, direct your team to eat those types of food. On this checklist, document what you will be serving, who will provide the food, and when it will be served. It's best to make the food available and let people eat prior to starting the meeting. Factor in about ten minutes for people to nosh on the snacks before beginning. This gives people time to ease into the environment and get to know each other in a more casual setting, rather than jumping right into the negotiation. Breaking bread together is a nice way to develop a sense of camaraderie before starting the discussion.

## Handouts

This section makes sure that you have all the materials you need during the negotiation. On this part of the form, document what you need, who is creating/providing it, and when they will have it ready. For formal and important negotiations, it's a good idea to have everything ready several days ahead of time so you can practice the introduction and presentation of it in the anticipated flow of your negotiation.

## Meeting Tools

It's a good idea to play classical music during meetings. It helps people stay relaxed and focused. Provide toys that people can use to have something to do with their hands; this will help lower anxiety. We've also found that mints have an impact on keeping

**Figure 4.2** Negotiation Meeting Checklist

Location: _____ Date: _____

Start – End Time: _____

| Participant | Reason for Participation | Phone Number | E-mail | Participation Confirmed |
|---|---|---|---|---|
| | | | | |
| | | | | |
| | | | | |
| | | | | |
| | | | | |
| | | | | |
| | | | | |
| | | | | |
| | | | | |

## Food

What: _____Who: _____

Contact Information: _____

*(continued on p. 73)*

*Figure 4.2* (continued from p. 72)

When Served:_____

## Restroom Locations

Men _____ Women _____

## Handouts

What is needed? _____

Who is creating? _____

When are they providing them? _____

## Meeting Tools

- ○ CD Player
- ○ Yo-Yos and Slinkys
- ○ Clock
- ○ Markers
- ○ Post-Its
- ○ Name Tags
- ○ Overhead Projector
- ○ LCD Panel
- ○ Phone

- ○ Classical Music CDs
- ○ Mints
- ○ Flip Chart
- ○ Note Paper
- ○ Pens
- ○ Tape
- ○ Transparencies
- ○ Laptop

## Internet Connection

- ○ Required
- ○ Not required

- ○ Other: _____

people relaxed. Make sure you have an adequate supply of sugar-free mints for the meeting. It's important that there is a wall clock in the meeting room so everyone can see what time it is — this will help to maintain momentum. If you're going to be doing brain-storming activities with the negotiating parties, consider having flip-chart paper, Post-It notes, markers, tape, and pens. Provide name tags if you have a large group of people who don't know each other. If people are making formal presentations, make sure you have the tools necessary for them to present — either a laptop with an LCD projector or an overhead projector. Assess whether you need a lap-top with an Internet connection to access important information. Also, consider if it will be important for you to have a phone to con-tact people not present in the meeting. If you can only use a cell phone, make sure it is in range in the meeting room. Paying at-tention to all of these details will ensure that the negotiation will run as smoothly as possible. Figure 4.2 is a reproduction of a ne-gotiation checklist that we've found helpful.

## APPLY IT

### Activity 1
Create a worksheet like table 4.1 to record your results. Take five minutes every morning to reflect on how you used one of these techniques to stay calm in a situation that would've normally set you off.

### Activity 2
Create a table like 4.2 in your notebook and identify six different negotiations, your role, and the skill you exhibited playing this role.

 **REFLECT**
When you are done, review the examples and see how your work compares. What was the most challenging for you?

Give a short summary (in three words or less) of your perceptions of the work you did for this chapter. You will remember more about what you did if you can attach a succinct message with some emotion to what you just experienced.

Identify three things you learned in this chapter.

## Examples from Our Students

### Reflect — What Did I Learn?

- Relaxation techniques. When I took the PMP class with Cheetah a few months ago, I loved the relaxation techniques. When I find myself in a situation that is stressful or I am experiencing stress, the breathing and stretching is very helpful.
- What techniques can be used to develop your own mood and the participants' mood for negotiations.
- Understanding that certain behaviors and routines will help me be more relaxed when dealing with difficult situations.
- Since I've completed this section, I've already incorporated the role/hat exercise into my planning and observations. It is interesting to observe the different roles each person plays during the process.

### ACT

Identify three things you're going to do differently in your next negotiation by understanding how to create the backdrop for the negotiation.

Since learning is a lifelong pursuit, identify three skills you want to improve because of what you learned in this chapter.

## Examples from Our Students

### Act — What Will I Do Differently?

- Use relaxation techniques to stay calm and in control as the discussion progresses.
- Try to prepare myself better with different techniques, like breathing exercises, the count-to-ten technique, etcetera.
- Switch hats (roles) during negotiations.
- Use relaxation techniques at different stages in the negotiation process.
- Stay in control of myself.
- Find ways to release stress quietly while in face-to-face situations.
- Become better at wearing the red hat.
- Master different roles and practice them prior to negotiations.

There are many things that go into preparing the backdrop for any negotiation. From preparing yourself emotionally and physically to determining what role(s) you will need to play, much of the work in the negotiation occurs before two parties ever meet face to face. Also, note the importance of the physical setting and all of the seemingly minor details that play a major part in the event. A well-prepared negotiator will move toward success fast, just like a Cheetah.

*Section Three*
# The Plot

Now, as they say, the plot thickens. While we've made careful preparations for our negotiation play, there are still twists and turns of the plot to take into account. That is what we'll discuss in this section. First, we'll examine the role of commitment in your negotiation. In the next chapter we'll visit the wild world of human nature and our sometimes subconscious reactions in negotiation situations. Then we will identify common negotiation tactics, how to recognize them, and when to use them.

*If with permission you ask*
*Commitment is truly your task*
*Then we shall see*
*It's smooth to agree*
*And get results that really do last*

# Chapter Five

# Scenes in the Negotiation Play

*I*n this chapter you will learn the value of commitment and asking permission to gain commitment to your objectives. Commitment will help you and the other party focus on the issues at hand and move through the negotiation fast. Understanding human nature can give you the self-awareness to keep you from unknowingly compromising or falling into typical sales traps. Knowing common negotiation tactics will save you time; you'll know not to play out those dramas.

## THE FIVE SCENES

There are five standard scenes in every negotiation play. While each negotiation is different with respect to the outcome, the process is the same, whether you are consciously aware of the steps or not. You can move a negotiation along faster and more effectively if you are conscious of those steps. Following this process also engenders commitment from the other party to

*Table 5.1* Scenes in the Negotiation Play

| Scene | Goal |
|-------|------|
| Planning | Making sure the necessary people are present in order to reach an agreement |
| Introduction | Allowing each side the opportunity to introduce their needs, wants, and issues |
| Bargaining | Exploring solutions and finding options for mutual gain |
| Agreement | Ironing out the terms, formalizing commitment |
| Closure | Determining the steps to start |

interact with you on your terms in a more positive and less adversarial negotiation setting.

The act of entering into a negotiation with someone assumes that there are issues that you need to explore so as to come up with alternative solutions. A negotiation is not a situation in which the decision is a done deal, where one party is the "winner" and gets what they want and the other party acquiesces just to move on. We've scoured the popular literature on negotiations and have found that some of the shorter books still view negotiation as a win-lose deal. The method we present is adapted from the ideas asserted in the book *Getting to Yes*, which views negotiation as an opportunity for mutual gain by all parties at the table. The process presented here will enable you to move the dialogue in your negotiation to the mutual gain orientation, even if the parties you are negotiating with initially view the negotiation as a win-lose interaction.

The best way to get people to engage with you in this process is to ask their permission. This acknowledges their involvement in a positive way, gains commitment commensurate with the stage of the negotiation, and can engage even contentious parties in a more positive and solution-oriented dialogue. People do not like to be viewed as inconsistent. Therefore, if you can get them to commit to engage with you in a positive negotiation style early on, they will be more likely to work through things with you when you run into areas in which you have less agreement.

Some "experts" view asking permission as a sign of weakness. We are not talking about asking for approval — that is different. Asking for permission in this context is a commitment-gaining move that is executed from a position of strength, not subservience.

The following are examples of permission-asking statements designed to develop deepening levels of commitment at each phase of a negotiation. Once you get into the actual negotiation, your questions may vary from these examples. The point here is that you want to ask the other party's permission to deepen their level of commitment to anything on which you agree. It also serves to engage them in committing to workable solutions for your negotiation issues.

## Scene 1: Planning

Planning — means making sure the necessary people are present in order to reach an agreement.

### Permission-Based Questions

- **I'm drafting an initial meeting agenda. Would you like to see it and provide input?**
  Very rarely will anyone refuse and if they do, they have in fact given you approval to set the agenda. Most frequently they will have one or two small changes, if any. The reality is that most people are just too busy to give much input. Just by asking this question, you've gotten their commitment for you to set an agenda.

- **Have we invited all the people we need at this meeting to close this issue?**
  Whatever way this is answered gives you the information you need to get commitment to have all the right people at the meeting to close this issue.

## Scene 2: Introduction

In the introduction scene, allow each side the opportunity to introduce their needs, wants, and issues.

### Permission-Based Questions

- **Is it okay with you if we follow the agenda and the process we originally agreed upon?**
  You're implying here that they agreed to the agenda when you gave them the option to review. If they have other ideas on how the meeting should progress, which they may not have fully articulated, now is also the time to get those out and agree to the process of the meeting. If they can commit with you to a process for the meeting, it will be easier to get them to commit to an agreement further into the negotiation.

- **What are your costs associated with not coming to an agreement today?**
  They may or may not answer this question. Essentially you're asking them the cost of their BATNA. This will give you the ZOPA — that is, the zone of possible agreement between their walk away and your walk away. Also, it's best to frame it this way because your subconscious does not hear the word "no," but instead it hears "come to an agreement today."

## Scene 3: Bargaining

In the bargaining scene you are exploring solutions and finding options for mutual gain.

### Permission-Based Questions

- **Are you open to hearing some ideas that can benefit both of us?**

  This question gets their okay for you to present your ideas. By framing it in the positive — that the ideas will benefit both of you — it increases your chances of getting an affirmative. Their positive go ahead also states that they are agreeing that your ideas are beneficial to them. It increases their commitment to your suggestions. Additionally, if you go first you are setting your benchmark. Do your work on the ZOPA and shoot very high on your aspirations of what you want for the ideal outcome.

- **Can I propose a solution?**

  By answering this question, they are committing to moving to the solution phase of the negotiation. You can propose a solution that improves your BATNA and diminishes their BATNA. If the other party asks why you've proposed your solution, always use the word because. It is irrelevant what follows the word because.

  For example: I propose to sell you a car for $25,000, which is $5,000 above the Blue Book value. You ask why I'm asking so much above Blue Book, and I say, "Because the car was very well cared for and has brand new tires." This is called anchoring your ZOPA. In this case the ZOPA is that you both perceive value in having a car that is well cared for with new tires. In reality, new tires and the fact that I think the car was well cared for does not change the Blue Book value of the car.

- **Which option do you prefer — A or B?**
  When you give people choices, they feel as though they had a say in the matter. Once they have made a choice, they have also made a commitment. For example, with the car — "The car is $25,000 without these floor mats, but I'll throw in the floor mats for an extra $500. They are worth $1,000, but because I can't use them and I'll have to take time to sell them separately, I'll throw them in." This gives you something to negotiate on as well when they start dickering on the price.

  This means if you propose that the car is worth $25,000 and the person comes back with, "Well I think it's only worth $18,000 because it has high mileage," you can counter offer with $24,500, then $24,250, then $24,125 — you aren't going down in $500 increments every time and it will appear that you are making concessions. Do not make unilateral concessions; take away something every time you drop the price and give reasons. Also label the concessions and appeal to being fair about your concessions. Justifying your claims regarding your initial price as well will increase their perception of the worth.

  If you are competing with other vendors on a contract, a good strategy once you get to the bargaining stage and you know that other vendors have underbid you, say, "We really want your business and we don't want to make this about price. We know you would prefer to have us as your vendor for reasons A, B, and C. What price do we have to meet to win this contract?" These statements followed by the question include two influence strategies. First, you're asking for the business, and people who ask for the business usually win the business. Second, they have essentially made a commitment to give you the business if they tell you the price you have to meet and you meet it.

## Scene 4: Agreement

Agreement is the scene for ironing out the terms and formalizing commitment.

### Permission-Based Questions

- **I'd like to propose an agreement — is this okay with you?**
  They are again committing to making an agreement. This moves you to closing the deal.

- **To make sure we get things right from your perspective, would you like to document the terms?**
  If you let them write out the agreement, they are much less likely to go back on any of the terms.

- **Are you sure you're comfortable with the terms of our agreement?**
  You want to make sure they are not just saying "yes, yes, yes" to get out of the negotiation situation, only to change their mind after they have left. Give them an opportunity to recommit to what you have agreed upon. Go back and revisit anything about which they may be uncomfortable. If you schedule your meeting close to lunch, or if they have to catch a plane or go to the restroom, you're more likely to get an affirmative.

## Scene 5: Closure

During closure, the parties determine the steps to start.

- **I'm more comfortable knowing the next steps. Can we outline them?**
  This makes sure that the nitty-gritty details of the agreement will be carried out once everyone leaves the table.

- **What is the best way for us to communicate with you once we leave this meeting?**
  This question ensures that they know you would like to keep the lines of communication open with respect to what you just agreed upon.

## MOVING THE NEGOTIATION ALONG

Prior to the negotiation, identify specific questions you can ask at each phase of the negotiation agenda to develop deeper levels of commitment. If you have other people participating in the negotiation, identify who is best suited for various stages of the process and make them the main participant in that section. In the previous chapter, you identified who was best suited to wear different hats in various aspects of a negotiation. Consider who should be doing the primary elements of each negotiation. You will not be sharing this document with the other party.

We complete a negotiation meeting agenda to share with the other party prior to the negotiation. The purpose of this is to start to engage the other party in a win-win negotiation in which you are both creating value. It includes information that you already collected elsewhere on your negotiation prep sheet (a document you will not share with the other party). The example below is an agenda that was created for a negotiation we did with a company we selected to partner with for servers to host our websites.

*Figure 5.1* Sample Negotiation Meeting Agenda

## CO-LOCATED SERVER PARTNERSHIP

Location: _Windsor Office_                Date: _2-14-05_

Start – End Time:  _9:00 am - 12:00 pm_

| Name | Purpose for Attending | Phone Number | E-mail |
|------|----------------------|--------------|--------|
| Michelle LaBrosse | She signs the check | 888-659-2013 | michelle @cheetahlearning.com |
| Rudi Mallant | He has to implement the solution with our clients | 888-659-2013 | rudi@cheetahlearning.com |
| Mark Click | He runs the company that provides the co-located server | 800-Go Serve | mark@serversrus.com |
| Bob Demarco | He runs the support department for the servers | 800-Go Serve | bob@serversrus.com |

*(continued on p. 90)*

*Figure 5.1* (continued from p. 89)

| Agenda Item | Goal | People Responsible | Time (From – To) |
|---|---|---|---|
| 1. Agenda Review | Agree to process of the meeting | Michelle | 9:00 – 9:15 |
| 2. Introductions of each party's negotiation objectives | Make sure both sides understand what they each need | Michelle | 9:15 – 9:45 |
| 3. Exploring Options | Find a solution of mutual gain | Rudi | 9:45 – 10:30 |
| 4. Developing Agreement Terms | Document solution | Mark | 10:45 – 11:30 |
| 5. Closure | Agree to the next steps | Michelle | 11:30 – 12:00 |

## APPLY IT

### Activity 1

Use the example in figure 5.1 to create your own agenda for a negotiation you are doing in the near future. Ask your counterpart if they would like to see this agenda and provide input. See what happens.

### Activity 2

Create your own permissions-based question worksheet and test it out. See what happens and how you can improve the way you interact while negotiating with counterparts.

 **REFLECT**

When you are done with these activities, review the example and see how your work compares. Give a short summary (in three words or less) of your perceptions of the activities. You will remember more about what you did if you can attach a succinct

**Table 5.2** Sample Permissions-Based Questions Worksheet

| Negotiation Stage | Permission-Based Questions | Who/Why |
|---|---|---|
| **Planning:** Making sure the necessary people are present in order to reach an agreement | Mark, would you like to review a proposed agenda? | Michelle/Leader — White Hat role |
| **Introduction:** Allowing each side the opportunity to introduce their needs, wants, and issues | Does everyone agree to the agenda? | Michelle/Leader — White Hat role |
| **Bargaining:** Exploring solutions and finding options for mutual gain | Can we explore some ideas now? I have a couple of ideas to share that will be beneficial to everyone. Would you like to hear them? | Rudi/Good Cop — Yellow Hat role |
| **Agreement:** Ironing out the terms, formalizing commitment | Are we ready to reach agreement? I'd like to propose an agreement — is this okay with everybody? | To make sure we document everything correctly, Mark or Bob, would you like to write it all down? |
| **Closure:** Determining the steps to start | I'm more comfortable knowing the next steps. Can we outline them? What is the best way to communicate once we leave this meeting? | Michelle/Coordinator — Blue Hat role<br><br>Rudi/Leader — White Hat role — He's the leader of the implementation and leadership is transferring to him from this point on. |

message with some emotion to what you just experienced. Identify three things you learned by practicing the scenes in the negotiation play.

## Examples from Our Students

### Reflect — What Did I Learn?
- Create negotiation plan before negotiating.
- The negotiation prep and practice is also a good tool going into a key session as it further refines the I want/they want exercise.
- Setting a proper environment, being organized, and documenting what I want to accomplish in each negotiation will help me have a more positive experience.

 **ACT**

Identify three things you're going to do differently in your next negotiation based on what you learned by understanding the scenes in the negotiation play.

Since learning is a lifelong pursuit, identify three skills you want to improve because of what you learned in this chapter.

## Examples from Our Students

### Act — What Will I Do Differently?
- Use the negotiation template to prepare myself better for the meetings.
- Allot time to consider logistics.
- Practice permission-based questions.
- Recognize the importance of the stage for the meeting — build the environment.
- Prepare for the meeting and all the phases.
- Invest enough time up front to be fully prepared for the meeting.

Asking permission-based questions is the best way to gain the other party's commitment to a positive process and outcome for your negotiation. Understanding how these types of questions are relevant at each of the five stages of a negotiation helps keep momentum going for fast and effective results. This chapter focused on positive techniques you can use in a negotiation to further advance the position of both parties. The next chapter focuses on human nature in negotiations, which will help you to understand both your own and others' motivations throughout the negotiation process.

*Human nature has rules all its own*
*Know them well, so you won't groan*
*When your reaction*
*Brings less satisfaction*
*From a response you feel that you've blown*

*Chapter Six*

# Human Nature in Negotiations

*M*uch of negotiations are a matter of influence and persuasion. Robert B. Cialdini, PhD, author of *Influence: The Psychology of Persuasion*, states,

"You and I exist in an extraordinarily complicated stimulus environment; easily the most rapidly moving and complex that has ever existed on this planet. To deal with it, we need shortcuts. We can't be expected to recognize and analyze all the aspects in each person, event, and situation we encounter in even one day. We haven't the time, energy, or capacity for it. Instead, we must very often use our stereotypes, our rules of thumb to classify things according to a few key features and then to respond mindlessly when one or another of these trigger features is present" (Cialdini, 7).

The point is that we need to be aware of our stereotypical social features, make conscious choices in our negotiations, and respond mindfully.

Here are some stereotypical ways people try to influence and persuade each other. Pay attention when these things happen in a negotiation — whether it's you or the other party making them happen.

## RECIPROCATION

When a person is given something, they feel obligated to reciprocate in turn. In negotiation, it is an important factor to be aware of: by first doing us a favor, others can increase the chance that we will comply with one of their requests. Note also that we tend to exhibit the obligation to receive, which makes this rule easy to exploit.

People selling time-share condos use this by inviting you to take a free vacation. In exchange, you have to attend a hard-sell presentation to purchase the time-share. This tactic is used more innocuously by organizations that "give" free personalized mailing labels when requesting a charitable donation. It is our human nature, and the factor of reciprocation, that benefits these enterprises.

Another demonstration of this factor is an obligation to make a concession to someone who has made a concession to us. Because the factor for reciprocation governs the compromise process, it is possible to use an initial concession as part of a highly effective compliance technique. The technique is a simple one that we call the *rejection-then-retreat technique*. Children are masters of this technique. Suppose you want me to agree to a certain request. One way to increase your chances would be first to make a larger request of me — one that I will most likely turn down. Then, after I have refused, you would make the smaller request that you were really interested in all along ("No, you can't have a horse but you can have a cookie"). Provided that you have structured your requests skillfully, I should view your second request as a concession of my own, the only one I would have immediately open to me — in compliance with your second request.

## Your Defense

Hard as it may be, we have to be aware of our nature and not allow the other party to apply this tactic because its force is very strong. Understand what is being presented as a gift or a genuine offer. If someone offers something, take the time to acknowledge it and understand the motive behind it. Reciprocate in kind — that is, give something of similar value back. When you get the free mailing labels, send them a pad of Post-Its.

## Your Advantage

Begin any meeting by giving everyone at the table a pen or some small gift. Make a concession on something meaningless early in the negotiation.

## COMMITMENT AND CONSISTENCY

The drive to be, and look, consistent constitutes a highly potent weapon of social influence, often causing us to act in ways that are clearly contrary to our own best interests. Inconsistency is commonly thought to be an undesirable personality trait. The person whose beliefs, words, and deeds don't match up may be seen as indecisive, confused, two-faced, or even mentally ill.

Because one of our shortcuts tells us it is in our best interests to be consistent, we easily fall into the habit of being automatically so, even in situations where it is not the sensible way to be. Blind consistency offers us a shortcut through the density of modern life. Signing up for surefire weight loss plans and get-rich-quick schemes are common examples of people grasping for easy solutions — even when logic and facts may point otherwise.

Consistency is strongly invoked once commitment is engaged. For example, let's say you take up that time-share condo operation while you're on that free vacation. Once you've committed, it's exploitable, because now you've proven you enjoy going on vacation to that location. This is one of the aspects they'll use to hard-sell you on the time-share. Another tool of commitment is the written word. Studies show that having customers, rather than salesmen, fill out a sales agreement prevents customers from backing out of their contracts. The more public or the greater the effort that goes into the commitment, the stronger it is. Remember, commitment is a motivation that can be a positive element in your negotiations as well.

### Your Defense

Understanding the situation and recognizing when consistency is likely to lead to a poor choice is often signified by that gnawing feeling in the pit of the stomach. It is important to determine if the reasons for making a decision are genuine or mere justifications. Listen to your gut here. Also, when you're being pressured to make a decision on the spot, stop and wait twenty-four hours before you decide.

### Your Advantage

The previous chapter showed how to gain deeper levels of commitment by asking permission-based questions. Follow this technique and people will respond.

### SOCIAL PROOF

Social proof is the factor that individuals want to be aligned with, something with which the general population agrees. This factor is evident in simple things like laugh tracks on sitcoms — no one likes them, but it creates the desired effect. Social proof has the strongest pull on people who are put into an unknown situation and look externally for clues on how to make a decision, hence the popularity of folks like the Gartner Group research reports.

## Your Defense

Make sure to verify any proof presented to you.

## Your Advantage

In the presentation of your issues, provide research reports that show your case. Also, it helps to show a list of other people who have used your approach and testimonials.

## LIKEABILITY

Cialdini's book, *Influence: The Psychology of Persuasion*, and Lieberman's book, *Get Anyone to Do Anything*, both indicate that one of the surest ways to get agreement is to be likeable. We are most likely to say yes to someone we like. When we find that someone thinks well of us, we are driven to find them more likeable too. Have you ever noticed how salesmen, and car salesmen in particular, will make a point of finding some common ground with you? Or compliment you? They are trying to establish grounds for a reciprocal affection, which could lead to a sale.

## Your Defense

Be aware of this tendency. Most people accurately label a salesman's "fake" smile and presentation.

## Your Advantage

There are things you can do to improve your likeability index:

1. Dress like the people you are negotiating with and mirror their behavior.
2. Make sure you eat a high-protein meal prior to the meeting — this will make you more relaxed and confident and thus more likeable.

3. When meeting people, don't immediately smile — pause just a moment and then give them a smile as if you're looking at a baby. This gives the impression that you are really happy to see them and that you are not doing the salesman "jerk smirk."
4. Also, when first meeting people, look them in the eye and hold the gaze for just a second longer than usual. This fosters a sense of intimacy and connection.
5. Do stretching exercises. People who are agile are seen as younger and more attractive and thus more likeable.

## MATTER OF AUTHORITY

In our over-stimulated environment we have come to use shortcuts in acknowledging authority and complying with it. Authority can be represented by titles or clothing in the business world. It can also be represented by the location of the office.

### Your Defense

Your defense to this element is to understand if this person is truly an expert by virtue of their experience. If so, how truthful and unbiased are they? Look beyond the costume to the person. Also, just because an authority says so, does not make it true. Question authority here, and recognize when you're being compliant because someone is posturing as an authority.

### Your Advantage

If the parties with whom you are negotiating are swayed by the perception of authority, make sure you hold the negotiation meeting in an impressive location. Emphasize your expertise, dress in a manner that will convey your authority, and make sure your business card represents a title commensurate with your authority representation. It only costs about thirty-five dollars to create business cards, so if you need a title to influence, change the cards.

## SCARCITY

One can actually have a physical reaction to the thought that any desirable item is very limited and may not be available to us. Have you ever noticed the ads that state, "Today only! Closeout Sale!"? This is intended to motivate us to buy sooner.

### Your Defense

Scarcity is a very strong influence, and our best defense once again is awareness. Acknowledge the gut feeling that arises. Take time to diagnose your reaction before choosing to move forward. This tactic is usually used in conjunction with one or several other influence techniques.

### Your Advantage

Your time truly is a scarce resource. Make sure your negotiation meeting has a strict timetable and that you have to be somewhere within a short time after the end of the meeting. Scheduling the meeting to end near lunch is a good way to use the "time is scarce" strategy to speed things along.

## APPLY IT

The way to learn the impact of influence factors is to notice the world around you and how people use all these elements every day to "influence" you. It's time to determine what factors are being used on you. Table 6.1 presents an example. Create your own worksheet in your notebook and notice the influence factors in your day-to-day life.

 **REFLECT**

When you are done with these activities, review the example and see how your work compares. Give a short summary (in three words or less) of your perceptions of the activities. You will remember more about what you did if you can attach a succinct message with some emotion to what you just experienced.

Identify three things you learned by understanding common influence strategies.

## Examples from Our Students

### Reflect — What Did I Learn?
- The best tactic is to be honest and build trust.
- Negotiation is not a one-way street.
- How human nature factors into negotiations.
- It was interesting to see that the influence of negotiations is all around us every day in all we do.

### ACT

Identify three things you're going to do differently in your next negotiation based on what you learned by assessing your response to everyday influences.

Since learning is a lifelong pursuit, identify three skills you want to improve because of what you learned in this chapter.

## Examples from Our Students

### Act — What Will I Do Differently?
- Ask permission-based questions in negotiations.
- Try to use the reciprocation tactics as suggested.
- I will review my learning materials on human nature so I can be aware when different traits are being exhibited and act accordingly.
- Be more aware of when I am being steered by others.
- Remember how human nature is used to manipulate us into a decision.
- Influence the opponents during negotiations.

**Table 6.1 Examples of Influence Factors**

| Factor | Your Experience and Observations |
|---|---|
| Reciprocation | In the grocery store's deli department they were serving samples of a baked potato soup. I didn't know where to purchase it nor was I told that was their objective. I just saw it as a gift. But I did spend longer in the grocery store so statistics will show that I probably spent more money there. |
| Consistency | The landlord of one of our facilities was trying to get us to sign a longer term lease than we wanted to or had in the past. He tried to influence us by challenging the stability of our operation which he knew would get us to act consistently with how stable and long-term we thought our operation was. However we knew, but did not share, that we weren't happy with the location and only wanted it for a short while longer while we found another place. |
| Commitment | My children were badgering me while I was busy answering e-mail on the computer. I have a tendency to say, "Yeah, yeah, yeah" when they are badgering me and I'm trying to get something else done. They took that to mean I had made a commitment to take them out to get ice cream. |
| Social Proof | I was reading the latest report on President Bush justifying his desire to invade Iraq and they cited that in the US, the number of those in favor were 2 to 1 to those opposed. I observed that over forty people in my own environment were really on the fence — not representative of the 2 to 1 ratio. |
| Likeability | I noticed an example that proves this point from the other side of the spectrum — that people who are rude, especially at meal times, are really not liked much at all. Common social courtesy and manners are crucial if people want to be liked. |
| Authority | I was at a beach that had a number of signs warning people about not going swimming because of strong currents, etc. However, there were quite a few people swimming with no problem in the water, and it looked quite calm. |
| Scarcity | I got an e-mail that told me I only had twenty-four hours to take advantage of this great offer to lose twenty pounds by Easter. I'm not sure if these e-mails really generate any sales, but they must if people keep sending them. |

- Stay detached so I can be more aware of others' motives.
- How to handle the reciprocate tactics when I am on the receiving side.

Being aware of the way human nature affects your ability to negotiate makes you a much more effective negotiator. It is important to understand the way others' actions affect us and to learn to use human nature to our advantage when we can. The next chapter deals with negative tactics that parties often use to make negotiations an adversarial, win-lose competition. We present information about such tactics and useful countermeasures you can implement to reduce their effects. Recognizing these negative tactics and refusing to be bullied by them is an essential part of successful, fast negotiations.

*There are tactics that some people will use*
*That are not intended to amuse*
*They may lie, cheat, and steal*
*But you'll stop the deal*
*And through the meeting you'll cruise*

## Chapter Seven

# Negotiation Tactics

*I*n this chapter we will cover various negotiation tactics. We've scoured the literature on this topic and combined our years of experiencing all types of adversarial and manipulative tactics at the hands of people with unscrupulous motives — from evangelical, proselytizing religious fanatics to the ubiquitous used car salesman. Our favorite in-depth summaries of negotiation and communication tactics are found in Tim Hindle's *Negotiating Skills*, David J. Lieberman's *Get Anyone to Do Anything*, and *Getting to Yes* by Roger Fisher and William Ury. The value of becoming familiar with these tactics is that as your awareness increases, the chances of being drawn into an emotional reaction decreases. Do not take these tactics personally. Be aware they are used for manipulative purposes and that by ignoring them and/or responding with nonviolent communication techniques, you'll neutralize the intended effect. After all, "A soft answer turneth away wrath" (Proverbs 15:1).

While most of these tactics can be addressed by your preparation and seeking permission and commitment, we all know people fall into their comfort zones and the unexpected may happen. Whatever you do, be prepared to fight these dirty bargaining tactics. You can be just as firm as they are — even firmer. It is easier to defend principle than an illegitimate tactic. Don't be a victim.

In our presentation of countermeasures, we include a script for nonviolent communication tactics. We presented this idea in chapter 4. The basic script for a nonviolent communication response is:

1. Observe rather than evaluate.
2. Express your feelings.
3. Acknowledge needs and responsibility for your feelings.
4. Express requests in terms of concrete actions.

The Center for Non-Violent Communications, www.cnvc.org, has given us permission to reprint their list of feelings and needs statements. When using these techniques, if you can capture the nuance of your feeling, you have far better success with achieving the goal of keeping all parties focused on objectives rather than positions and can more easily defuse harmful negotiation tactics.

Some examples of feelings you may experience when your needs are satisfied include compassion, enthusiasm, delight, confidence, satisfaction, or rejuvenated. On the other hand, when your needs are not satisfied, you may feel apathetic, miserable, frustrated, outraged, tense, or bewildered. To better understand when your needs are and are not being met, it helps to have a list of needs as a starting point. Perhaps you are seeking acceptance, equality, harmony, safety, or independence. Please see the appendix for a complete list of feelings and needs statements. It's important to understand the difference of

**Table 7.1** Observations with and without Evaluations

| With evaluations | Without evaluations |
|---|---|
| "You're never on time." | "In the last two weeks, you've been late four times." |
| "He's ugly." | "His looks do not appeal to me at all." |
| "You're always too busy to talk to me." | "I've tried to talk to you three times this week and each time you put me off." |

observations with and without evaluations. Let's look at a few examples.

The best way to deal with negative negotiation tactics is to be aware when they are being used and to know what type of countermeasures you can use to diffuse them. Table 7.2 provides a short summary of these tactics and countermeasures. Because this knowledge is so useful in negotiations, we then present each tactic in more detail, describing examples of negotiation tactics, the actions and words that indicate each tactic is in use, and specific countermeasure suggestions.

## NEGOTIATION TACTIC — MAKING THREATS

### Indicators
Negative repercussions if you fail to comply.

### Countermeasures
Inform the party you will not negotiate under duress and that you need to focus on outcomes for mutual gain. A nonviolent communication statement is to say, "I hear that you are saying there will be negative repercussions if I don't comply. I feel anxious about your statement. I need to focus on a situation that is

*(continued on p. 112)*

**_Table 7.2_** Negotiation Tactics, Indicators, and Countermeasures

| Negotiation Tactic | Examples of Indicators | Countermeasures |
|---|---|---|
| Making Threats | Cites negative repercussions if you fail to comply. | Do not negotiate under duress; focus on outcomes for mutual gain. |
| Insults | Questions your party's competence; uses destructive criticism. | Use a calming technique and restate your position; acknowledging insults explicitly will probably prevent a reoccurrence. |
| Bluffing | Threatens punitive action; makes doubtful assertions. | Question statements; ask for evidence to support their claims. |
| Intimidation | Makes you uncomfortable; keeps you waiting. | Keep to your terms or reschedule; identify objectionable circumstances and raise the issue with the other side. |
| Divide and Conquer | Tries to create dissension on your team. | Your negotiation prep should circumvent this tactic; call an adjournment if your team shows differing opinions. |
| Leading Questions | Asks questions that lead you to their opinion or stand. | Do not answer questions you do not know the purpose of; be willing to ask for clarification on claims or anything else you do not understand. |
| Emotional Appeals | Accuses you of being unfair or of lacking trust in them. | Circumvent by getting permission and commitment to your solution. Ask questions to validate their claims and remind them to work on the interest and not the position. |
| Testing Boundaries | Works on small and seemingly innocuous concessions that add up. | Circumvent by having a clear statement of your objectives. |

*(continued on p. 111)*

*Table 7.2* (continued from p. 110)

| Negotiation Tactic | Examples of Indicators | Countermeasures |
|---|---|---|
| Lying | Overstates experience or functionality. | Test truthfulness by asking questions. |
| Closed-Minded | Unable or unwilling to consider other options. | Provide additional information; use reciprocation; search for objective criteria. |
| Authority Issues | Does not have the authority to close the deal. | Consider which issues can be resolved with the people present; reschedule negotiation. |
| Good Cop/Bad Cop | People in other party play opposing roles. | Remember your objectives and use detachment techniques. |
| Extreme Demands | Begins with an extreme proposal to lower your expectations. | Bring this tactic to their attention and ask for principled justification. |
| Escalating Demands | Raises a demand for every concession they make; keeping score. | Call a break to stop momentum and proceed with restating your principles. |
| Hardhearted Policy | Seems willing but cites their boss or company policy as unbending. | Ask to have the right authority present to perform this negotiation to an agreeable conclusion; do not proceed. |
| Calculated Delay | Tries to delay conclusion until a time they believe is more favorable to them. | Look for objective conditions that can be used to establish a deadline and stick to them. |
| Take It or Leave It | Rules out interactive decision-making. | Change the subject; ask permission to explore alternative solutions. Continue to pursue options for mutual gain. |

mutually beneficial to continue with this negotiation. How would you like to proceed?"

## NEGOTIATION TACTIC — INSULTS

### Indicators

Questioning you or your company's competence or using destructive criticism. They may refuse eye contact.

### Countermeasures

Use a calming technique and restate your position and the need to achieve mutual gain. In each case, recognizing the tactic will help nullify its effect; bringing it up explicitly will probably prevent a reoccurrence. A nonviolent communication tactic is to say, "I hear you saying that you consider me XYZ (the insult). I am concerned. Is this perception going to impact our negotiation?"

## NEGOTIATION TACTIC — BLUFFING

### Indicators

Threatening punitive action or making doubtful assertions. You can recognize a bluffing tactic because they will generally overcompensate for their bluff by appearing to be completely behind their conviction. True confidence speaks for itself.

### Countermeasures

Question statements and ask for evidence to support their claims. A nonviolent communication tactic is to say, "I hear you saying XYZ. I need additional data to make a more informed decision. How can I get this data?"

## NEGOTIATION TACTIC — INTIMIDATION

### Indicators

Making you uncomfortable, keeping you waiting, meeting in an inappropriate setting, or taking calls/visitors during your negotiation.

### Countermeasures

Be aware of this tactic and keep to your terms or reschedule. If you are on their ground, it is up to you to identify objectionable circumstances and raise the issue with the other side. A nonviolent communication tactic is to say, "I see you are taking phone calls. I feel distressed that I took the time to make this meeting. I need to continue this discussion when we can both focus on the topic without interruptions. What would you suggest?"

## NEGOTIATION TACTIC — DIVIDE AND CONQUER

### Indicators

Trying to create dissension on your team by appealing to one of your members to be sympathetic to their side.

### Countermeasures

Your negotiation prep should circumvent this tactic; call an adjournment if your team shows differing opinions. A nonviolent communication tactic is to say, "I hear that people on my team have differing opinions. I feel puzzled and I need to spend some time alone with my team to understand our issues. Please give us a couple of minutes to have a private conversation."

## NEGOTIATION TACTIC — LEADING QUESTIONS

### Indicators

Asking questions that lead you to their opinion or stand.

## Countermeasures

Do not answer questions that you do not know the purpose of. Be willing to ask for clarification on claims or anything you do not understand. A nonviolent communication tactic is to say, "I hear that you have asked me XYZ. I don't quite understand this question. Can you please clarify why you need to know this?"

## NEGOTIATION TACTIC — EMOTIONAL APPEALS

### Indicators
Accusing you of being unfair or of lacking trust in them.

### Countermeasures
Should be circumvented by asking permission-based questions and getting a commitment to your solution. Ask questions to validate their claims and remind them to work on the interest and not the position. A nonviolent communication tactic is to say, "I heard you state that you think we are being unfair. I feel apprehensive about interacting on this emotional issue. I need to reconnect with the overall objectives for our negotiation. Can you help me better understand your objectives and priorities?"

## NEGOTIATION TACTIC — TESTING BOUNDARIES

### Indicators
Working on small and seemingly innocuous concessions that add up.

### Countermeasures
This should be circumvented by having a clear statement of your objectives. A nonviolent communication tactic is to say, "We have conceded on XYZ. I am reluctant to continue. I need to better understand our mutual objectives. Can you recap our end goal?"

## NEGOTIATION TACTIC — LYING

### Indicators

Overstating experience or functionality. For example, the other side states they have ten years of experience with a relatively new software program.

### Countermeasures

You may test their truthfulness by inventing a false fact. For example, you may say, "A couple years ago we were shut down for a week when we upgraded to the new version of the software," and watch their reaction. If they hesitate and agree, you can be certain they're lying. If they immediately respond, "I don't recall anything like that," you can be certain they are truthful. Be sure to separate the people from the problem. A nonviolent communication tactic is to say, "I hear you saying that you have ten years of experience with this program. I am perplexed because it's only been around for three years. I need to better understand your experience. Can you explain how you worked with the program for ten years?"

## NEGOTIATION TACTIC — CLOSED-MINDEDNESS

### Indicators

Unable, or unwilling, to consider other options.

### Countermeasures

Change their physiology. Get them to stand (assuming they're sitting) or move around the room. Provide additional information to give the party the option of changing their minds based on something concrete. Use reciprocation; adopt a two-sided argument that shows you understand and appreciate their position. Maybe the other party is personally attached to their opinion and attaches their identity to it. In this case, you must search for objective criteria; create a joint search for that criteria and what standards you use. Finally, never yield to pressure — only to principle. A nonviolent communication tactic is to say, "I hear you saying that approach X is the only thing you would consider. I am disappointed. I need to understand if there are any other approaches you would consider. Can we discuss this over a beer?" (The key is to come up with something to get them physically out of the room.)

## NEGOTIATION TACTIC — AUTHORITY ISSUES

### Indicators
The other side says they do not have the authority to make concessions or close the deal.

### Countermeasures
Although you asked this question up front with the agenda, things happen, and you will save time by confirming that you are sitting across the table from individuals who have the right authority. If you determine the right players are not present, you can decide how you wish to proceed. A nonviolent communication tactic is to say, "I see that you do not have the proper people here to make an ultimate decision. I feel frustrated. I need to make the best use of my time with our interaction. What issues can we resolve with the people present?"

## NEGOTIATION TACTIC — GOOD COP/BAD COP

### Indicators
One person from the other party will take a hard line with you while another will take a softer approach to appeal to you.

## Countermeasures

This is a very obvious technique and you need only fall back to your objectives and detachment techniques. A nonviolent communication tactic is to say, "I hear that you and your partner have different approaches. I am skeptical. I need to understand the objectives. Can you explain what you need to get out of this negotiation?"

## NEGOTIATION TACTIC — EXTREME DEMANDS

### Indicators

The other party starts out with an extreme proposal with the goal of lowering your expectations. It also has the effect of lowering their credibility.

### Countermeasures

Bringing this tactic to their attention and asking for principled justification of their proposal will bring the extreme demand to light. A nonviolent communication tactic is to say, "I see that you want XYZ. I feel confused. I need to understand the reasons why you want XYZ. Can you explain your rationale and justify the reason for your request?"

## NEGOTIATION TACTIC — ESCALATING DEMANDS

### Indicators

The other party raises a demand for every concession they make. It's called keeping score and they're hoping to make you agree quickly before they raise more demands.

### Countermeasures

You may call a break to stop momentum and proceed with restating your principles. A nonviolent communication tactic is to say, "I heard you ask for XYZ. I am concerned about this because my objective is X. I need to take a break to think about this."

## NEGOTIATION TACTIC — HARDHEARTED POLICY

### Indicators
The other party seems willing but cites their boss's or company's unbending policy.

### Countermeasures
You need to have the right authority to perform this negotiation to an agreeable conclusion; do not proceed. A nonviolent communication tactic is to say, "I hear that you cannot deviate from company policy. I am concerned about the viability of our negotiation. I need to understand the issues that you can resolve on your own within the boundaries of your company policy. Can we explore this?"

## NEGOTIATION TACTIC — CALCULATED DELAY

### Indicators
The other side would like to delay conclusion until a time they believe is more favorable to them.

### Countermeasures
Look for objective conditions that can be used to establish a deadline and stick to them. A nonviolent communication tactic is to say, "I hear that you would like to wait until X to make a decision. I feel impatient that we've come this far and now you want to wait. I need to know the steps to move this forward to come to a decision. Can we establish how we will decide on a firm deadline?"

## NEGOTIATION TACTIC — TAKE IT OR LEAVE IT

### Indicators

The other side proposes a solution and does not want to discuss any of the terms, basically saying, "Here's our offer. Take it or leave it."

### Countermeasures

This tactic negates the fact that you are negotiating, which means interactive decision-making. Consider ignoring it at first — change the subject or ask permission to explore alternative solutions. Don't let them feel they've painted themselves into a corner, and continue to pursue options for mutual gain. A nonviolent communication tactic is to say, "I hear that you are proposing to leave if we don't accept your offer. I feel perplexed because I thought we were in an interactive decision-making process. I need to understand other options before we just walk away. Can you explain the alternatives as you see them?"

### APPLY IT

Let's look at some examples of negative negotiation tactics that our students have experienced. This series of examples displays the tactic, the student's reaction, and the impact.

### Tactic — Calculated Delay

Had a manager who would schedule a meeting and then postpone it for days or weeks, then catch you off guard in the hallway and discuss what he wanted you to agree to.

### Reaction

Stated repeatedly that I was not prepared to make a decision on the spot and would then try to take a couple of days to think about it.

## Impact

Hurt our relationship.

## Tactic — Insults

One of my clients had a style of insulting those he worked with. His team members were afraid to work for him.

### Reaction

I had a different approach; I was challenged by his comments, and I confronted him respectfully.

### Impact

Result was positive; he was taken aback and I was treated well.

## Tactic — Authority Issues

The right person to make the decision wasn't there.

### Reaction

Tried to end the negotiation by stating that it is wasting the time of both the parties since the authority to make the agreement wasn't present.

### Impact

A more authoritative personality was included in the negotiation, capable of making the agreement based on the authoritative powers.

## Tactic — Bluffing

In working with a specific prestigious customer, if he did not get the answer that he wanted, then he threatened to bring in his attorneys.

## Reaction

Because he had shown this behavior in the past, I tried to present the facts and not get caught up in his emotional trauma.

## Impact

I am usually able to satisfy his request, and he continues to be our customer.

## Tactic — Intimidation

It was during my first car-buying experience. At the car dealership, the salesman asked for my keys to have my current car evaluated for a trade-in value. He then disappeared for thirty minutes even though I had told him I was on my lunch hour.

## Reaction

I was nervous about being late for work, which added to the car-buying pressure. I eventually bought a car from them but probably paid too much for it.

## Impact

It was a valuable learning experience. I now pull Blue Book values before I go into a dealership. I also go in with a prepurchase certificate from the dealer of my choice. That way I have more price bargaining power. If the salesman has a problem with any of my terms, I walk. There are hundreds of dealerships just waiting for a new customer.

## Tactic — Divide and Conquer

I had a new employee that wanted concessions granted to her because she couldn't seem to follow the rules that my other employees didn't have a problem with. She began to speak to my employees individually, trying to get them to challenge my authority. Several of them complained to me that she was disruptive and unpleasant to be around.

### Reaction
I counseled her regarding the group and job expectations, both of which she knew before taking the position. I let her know that she needed to comply with group rules or face the consequences. It was up to her. I also suggested that if I had further issues, we would both seek the advice of the HR department to remedy the situation.

### Impact
She is no longer an employee for this company.

## Tactic — Hardhearted Policy
I had a quote for an item from an online store. I went into a local retailer and was told the price would be twenty-five dollars higher.

### Reaction
I questioned the price difference. The store manager dismissed the online price saying that the online store didn't have overhead costs to consider. I asked for a list of these overhead costs and wasn't given an answer.

### Impact
I walked away without buying the item. I then obtained the names of the company's president and VP of customer service as well as the corporate address. I sent them an e-mail asking for their thoughts on this matter, inquiring if I had a mistaken point of view concerning this situation.

Two days later, I received a telephone call from the VP of customer service saying that I was absolutely right in my belief that the prices should be the same. She also stated that the manager mentioned in my e-mail had been "counseled" on the correct procedure should such an event occur in the future.

### Tactic — Testing Boundaries
A current vendor bad-mouthed a competitor's product that we were reviewing.

### Reaction
We went to see the other vendor's product and evaluated it ourselves.

### Impact
The act of looking at the competition's product resulted in better treatment from our existing vendor.

### Tactic — Intimidation
Buying a new car that offered an extended maintenance package.

### Reaction
The car dealer tried to make us feel stupid and incompetent for not wanting their extended maintenance.

### Impact
We held our ground and did not waver. The deal finally closed.

### Your Experiences
Now identify five situations in past negotiations in which you experienced one or several of these tactics. What was your reaction? How did it impact the negotiation? Record these in your notebook.

 **REFLECT**
When you are done with these activities, review the example and see how your work compares. In your notebook give a short summary (in three words or less) of your perceptions of

the activities. You will remember more about what you did if you can attach a succinct message with some emotion to what you just experienced.

Identify three things you learned by understanding negative negotiation tactics and the countermeasures you can use to neutralize them.

## Examples from Our Students

### Reflect — What Did I Learn?
- Be careful of others' negative tactics and refrain from using them.
- Asking the right questions can put me in a position of strength.
- Have a plan and cues to keep things on track. Use the yes funnel, even in project meetings.
- Permission-based questions help generate agreement.

 **ACT**

Identify three things you're going to do differently in your next negotiation based on what you learned by understanding negotiation tactics.

Since learning is a lifelong pursuit, identify three skills you want to improve because of what you learned in this chapter.

## Examples from Our Students

### Act — What Will I Do Differently?
- Look for negotiation tactics to lure me into making a decision that I am not ready for.
- I will review my negotiation tactics learning materials so that I can be aware when different techniques are being used and mitigate them.

- Always make sure we have the right players before entering a meeting.
- Be more aware of tactics.
- Try to be less reactive during the negotiation processes and remember that negotiation tactics are being used to force me into a decision.
- Mastering skills for asking permission-based questions.

Now you should be aware of many of the common negative negotiation tactics out there and the best way to deal with them. Understanding these tactics and knowing how to implement nonviolent communication will help you to achieve positive negotiation results, fast. Next we take a look at money and how different people's money issues affect their negotiation technique. Money can be a sensitive issue, but with the proper preparation you can quickly overcome the difficulties that money creates.

*Section Four*
# Curtains Up!

We are rehearsed, the scene is set, and the players are ready —
time for curtains up! The negotiation unfolds and the plot plays
out to what will hopefully be the happy ending. However, now
that the parties have found common ground and terms, we need
to talk money and get it all down in writing. And by the way, "hap-
pily ever after" only comes if you also make provisions for the in-
evitable changes that will come along.

*Isn't it really quite funny*
*How we all have reactions to money*
*What makes one fear*
*To another is dear*
*And makes someone else sick to their tummy*

# Chapter Eight

# Let's Talk Money

In this chapter, you will learn how to talk money after you have resolved your negotiation issues (that don't involve money). While the successful act of negotiation will get two parties to common ground for mutual gain, we need to move through terms and onto the topic of money. Much discomfort can accompany this topic, and you'll learn to tackle the topic objectively. As Sophocles wrote in *Antigone*, "Money: There's nothing in the world so demoralizing as money" (Bartlett's, 67).

The more you talk money, the easier it gets. And the more data you collect prior to talking money, the easier it is yet. One of the first questions in the negotiation play is not so much *how* to talk money, but *when*. It is best to start talking money after you agree to the specific issues on the table. However, you can, and must, collect data on the financial aspects of the issues well before your negotiation meeting. The rule of thumb is "In God we trust — for all others, collect data." As described in chapter 6, the influence factors associated with collecting financial data to more effectively talk money are social proof and authority.

How you talk money also depends on with whom you are negotiating. Table 8.1 lists standard money-talk issues along with the different relationships you may have in your professional and personal life. It also illustrates the type of data to collect ahead of time in order for you to be best prepared to talk money. There are numerous websites out there that offer labor rates and salary data — some require a fee. Do your homework!

In negotiations, things can fall apart fast when one or both parties have "issues" about money. In personal relationships, all the issues can quickly become about "money" to mask dealing with other equally serious issues. But it doesn't have to be this way — if even one party knows how to defuse the emotional issues many people have about money. Table 8.2 covers sample money issues that may come up during a negotiation in various professional and personal relationship configurations. It includes techniques to defuse people's triggers on what can be a touchy subject for some. To be effective in negotiating issues about money, it's critical that you understand and release your own emotional issues around money. Following this table is a series of questions to get you thinking about your own money issues.

## NEGOTIATION PREP SHEET FOR MONEY ISSUES

Prior to each negotiation you enter, identify the possible money issues that may come up for either you or the other party. Also, identify how you can prepare ahead of time to discuss them and how you can respond during the actual negotiation to defuse money issues.

**_Table 8.1_** Relationships with Corresponding Money Talk and Influence

| Relationships | Money Talk | Influence Factors |
|---|---|---|
| Team Member | Compensation — Salary, bonus, consulting contracts | Salary surveys, industry standard labor rates, company standards, HR policies |
| Supervisors | Project budgets, salary compensation | Task estimates, labor rates, material estimates, cost of capital, salary surveys |
| Sales Representatives | Submitting RFPs and RFQs | Cost comparisons (get multiple bids) |
| Customers | Answering RFPs and RFQs | Provide cost comparisons, expected monetary value analyses, standard bid sheets, standard rate sheets, standard quote sheets |
| Spouses, Children, and Parents | Family budget, vacation expenses, retirement planning, car and home purchases, educational expenses, use of credit, gift giving, recreational items, lifestyle purchases | Influence factors in personal relationship with respect to money are more complex because they can involve an entire set of unstated expectations embedded in personal relationships. That said, typically the person who makes the money has more influence in how that money is used. |

Table 8.3 presents examples of money issues we've encountered in our jobs. We highlight our data-collection activities and the methods we used to defuse these issues. When preparing for a negotiation, identify prospective money issues and how you can influence and defuse them.

**_Table 8.2_ Examples of Money Issues and Defusers**

| Relationship | Issues | Defusers |
|---|---|---|
| Subordinate Team Member | 1.Not enough money to complete the project work.<br>2.Not getting adequately compensated for the work they are doing. | 1.Find out what they can complete in budget.<br>2.Find out the industry standard for compensation. Learn whether there are qualified people who will work for the compensation level. Find out if you can get more money to compensate them. Tie compensation into some level of remunerated performance so they make money when the project develops an ROI. |
| Sponsor | 1.Not having enough money in the budget to meet the scope of a project.<br>2.Not trusting the data provided by the manager about the real cost of the project (fear of bait-and-switch tactic). | 1.Find a scope that will fit budget.<br>2.Lay out the entire project with the work breakdown structure (WBS), deliverables, schedule, and budget in a very succinct format that a sponsor can understand. |

*(continued on p. 133)*

## YOUR MONEY ISSUES

Money has as many meanings as there are people. Your own feelings about money may actually be holding you back from being an effective negotiator. Remember one of the key factors for success in a negotiation is being detached. It's hard for many people to get detached when the subject of money comes up — especially if it's their own company and the negotiation is affecting their bottom line. There is a standard saying in sales that you have to act like you don't need the money. In personal relationships, money

*(continued on p. 136)*

*Table 8.2* *(continued from p. 132)*

| Relationship | Issues | Defusers |
|---|---|---|
| Customer | 1. Not willing to pay what it's really going to take to do the project.<br>2. Telling you that they have another company who can do it for a lot less money.<br>3. Asking for payment terms. ("I can't afford to pay you all at once.")<br>4. Past history of slow or nonpayment. | 1. Find out what they are willing to pay.<br>2. Decide if you're going to negotiate on price or value. Find out if the other company is bidding on the same thing you are (they may not be). Assess how important this client really is.<br>3. Determine if your customer can really afford your services or products (i.e., qualify them).<br>4. Get a good portion of the money up front. Only extend purchase orders to qualified customers. |
| Sales Representative | 1. Buying in — This means dramatically underbidding the contract to get the job with the hopes of recouping on the back end with other products and services.<br>2. Low balling the job or product. (Low balling means prices that are substantially lower than the industry standard.)<br>3. Padding the job bid or the cost of the product. | 1. Ask to see data on how they developed their bid. Get a full description of their products and services. CAREFULLY read the fine print on any standard boilerplate to make sure bid is inclusive.<br>2. Ask for a product and a price guarantee. Make sure to check their references. Make sure the product or service meets your specifications.<br>3. Know your spending limit ahead of time and what things should cost. Ask for references and documentation about how they came up with their prices. Give them time to go back and revise their bid. |

**_Table 8.3_ Sample Money Issues and Defusers**

| Money Issue | Who/Relationship | Data Collection (Influence) | Defusers |
|---|---|---|---|
| Price of co-locating server — buy in suspected. | Sales representative for a company who was going to host our web server. | Collected standard bid sheets for the same service from five other sources. We knew what this should cost. | Asked them for clarification of what was included in their bid. They resubmitted the proposal three times before we finally accepted it because of their emphasis on their guarantee. The reason for their low bid price was actually due to economies of scale — they could afford to charge less than their competitors and still make a profit because they ran their business more efficiently. |
| Salary of a key subordinate team player — wanted more compensation. | Subordinate team member. | Found compensation factors that would influence them other than salary — such as vacation time, flexible hours, choice of project tasks. | Acknowledged value and worth of team member prior to presenting alternative compensation proposal. Included an incentive compensation portion based on ROI of their individual efforts. |

_(continued on p. 135)_

*Table 8.3* (continued from p. 134)

| Money Issue | Who/Relationship | Data Collection (Influence) | Defusers |
|---|---|---|---|
| Offered a very well-funded three month contract to develop a one-time customized product. | Customer | Analyzed how it would impact our overall business. | Since we didn't want to alienate a potential client we had to find a way to politely decline the request for our help since it was outside the strategic direction for the business. Pointed them in the direction of other resources that would do a very good job for them. |
| One parent who pays 95% of expenses for children gets sued by noncustodial parent for custody. Parent suing wants to get children for the child support payments and to be relieved of having to pay the current small amount of child support. Parent suing claims custodial parent is unstable but has no data to validate this charge. | Ex-spouse | Get data that validates the stability of the custodial parent. Review existing financial situation of both parties. | Identify what is affordable for the noncustodial parent regardless of what is "fair" with respect to sharing the costs for raising the children. Identify prosecuting parent's issues about how the children are being raised and address those separately from the child support issues. |

is typically used to control the "power" of the relationship. You have to become detached from the whole discussion about money during a negotiation to be successful.

Saying this is one thing, but doing it is completely different. The following six questions are designed to get you thinking about your personal issues about money so you can better detach yourself from your own money issues. If you are not comfortable with this topic, please do not feel as if you have to share your answers with anyone. Answer these questions with the first thing that pops into your head. Give yourself five minutes to run through all the questions — you'll get much better answers this way than if you sit around for hours contemplating them. If you do choose to share your answers, make sure you do it with someone you can trust to keep them confidential.

1. Have you ever been scared about money? If so why? Are you scared about money now?
2. What power does having money give you? Can something other than money give you that power?
3. What thrills you about money?
4. If you had enough money to be financially secure the rest of your life (for some that is several thousand dollars, for others it is several hundred million), what would you be doing right now?
5. What did answering these first four questions teach you regarding your feelings about money?
6. How would you like to feel about money?

## APPLY IT

In your notebook, identify money issues you've encountered in the past and analyze how you could have better handled them. See table 8.3 for an example.

**REFLECT**

When you are done with these activities, review the example and see how your work compares. Give a short summary (in three words or less) of your perceptions of the activities. You will remember more about what you did if you can attach a succinct message with some emotion to what you just experienced.

Identify three things you learned by assessing money issues.

## Examples from Our Students

### Reflect — What Did I Learn?

- The key to concluding a successful negotiation is to confront money issues head on.
- I learned that money matters, and I learned the factors that affect money negotiations.
- The more information gathered in advance of discussing the money element, the more smoothly the contracting process will be.
- How to use a defuser strategy to manage people's triggers when discussing money.

**ACT**

Identify three things you're going to do differently in your next negotiation based on what you learned by assessing money issues. Since learning is a lifelong pursuit, identify three skills you want to improve because of what you learned in this chapter.

## Examples from Our Students

### Act — What Will I Do Differently?

- I will remember that it usually has nothing to do with the people involved. As much as I want to believe it's about the people, it's really about the money. I will remember that.

- Think through the closure and money aspects in more detail prior to a meeting.
- If I'll be dealing with money matters, I'll prepare with the stress factors and defusers.
- Prepare for the meeting dealing with money matters.
- Won't let agreement slip away due to lack of attacking money issues and concerns head on. Use permissions to build the yes funnel to close these issues and concerns.
- Practice separating money from emotion.

Once you have successfully maneuvered through the money issues, you are approaching the end of the negotiation. The next step is to get everything down in writing and create a formal contract that records the terms of your negotiation. This step is very important because it will seal the deal and set the plan in motion for you to get moving fast.

*There once was a paper called contract*
*That struck fear in hearts that it contact*
*Agreements in writing*
*Can be quite exciting*
*Cuz now you know fiction from fact*

*Chapter Nine*

# Agreements, Attorneys, and the Afterlife

*I*t is now time to capture the fruit of our negotiation — to put the terms and the money into one place called an agreement or contract. Typically, this formal document is carefully structured by legal departments or attorneys, and so most likely you will, and should be, using boilerplate contracts. These are standard contracts that are already crafted, in which you simply fill in the blanks. If you don't have a boilerplate contract now, make sure you have one prior to entering into any negotiation, as it will significantly speed things along. Completing the contract is a critical step in completing the negotiation. If you have to have numerous contracts sent back and forth, your negotiation will drag on longer than necessary. For many of the negotiations that most people face in their day-to-day work life, boilerplate contracts suffice quite well.

## AGREEMENTS

According to E. Thorpe Barrett's *Write Your Own Business Contracts:*

*What Your Attorney Won't Tell You*, all contracts at the minimum must include the following information:

- **Identification of the parties to the agreement.** This is the who's who of your agreement. It is usually apparent from the terms of agreement, but individuals should be identified by name and any other description, if possible.

- **Consideration.** This means each party must gain something from the agreement. It must be written into the agreement what each party will provide.

- **Terms of the agreement.** This is the meat of the agreement, which lists in clear language exactly who does what, when, and so on. This is the part that should get most of the attention and detail. [Note: If you structure your agreement using a project agreement similar to the one presented in our book, *Cheetah Project Management*, you can use much of the work that you have already done for that to create your contract. The Cheetah Project Management Project Agreement template is included for your use in the appendix of that book. We do recommend that you get the book, *Cheetah Project Management*, to best implement any project agreements you create.]

- **Execution of the agreement.** This means both parties must sign the agreement, making sure the one who signs has the proper authority to do so.

- **Delivery of the agreement.** This means the executed agreement must be given to each of the parties.

Like ice cream, agreements come in a variety of flavors, depending on the agreement's purpose. For example, if you are a project manager, there is a pretty good chance that you may encounter the need to contract with a consultant. This flavor agreement would uniquely include some or all of the following elements:

- Any confidentiality issues
- Any warranty given by the consultant
- An outline of the change control process
- Assignment of patent rights, copyrights, or software developed
- Precisely what the consultant will do and when, including specifications and delivery
- How to handle the possibility of the consultant doing work for competing companies
- Enumeration of any liability to be assumed by consultant for products
- The terms of payment and whether you are using a fixed price or a time and materials cost structure, which will be reflected in your change control process

## ATTORNEY ALERTS

Attorneys may use the practice of "creeping" while drafting the agreement. This means that among the legalese they slant terms to be a little more favorable to their client. Being the one who creates the first draft can tilt this in your favor, so if you are not creating the initial draft, be aware of this practice.

Lawyers are not project managers, so it would be unwise to expect them to be. It is your duty to carefully monitor the activities of attorneys. There is no magic in the legal world. As with any other vendor, tell them specifically what you want, find out what it will cost, and keep track of the charges. Don't let them charge more for the big words!

Keeping in mind that there is no magic in the legal world, select your attorney as you would a vendor. Make use of referrals, references, and interviews, and don't forget to try speed-reading his or her personality. All of these tactics will help you to determine his or her integrity. Don't use a litigation specialist or a general practitioner to draft your business agreement. Be sure the attorney is proficient with the type of work you are procuring. It is common to pay a retainer rather than contingency funds. It may be useful to start out by giving a very small and specific task so that you can judge performance.

## AFTERLIFE

In any negotiation, there will be changes. How you plan to manage change control must be included in your boilerplate contracts. As a professional, you need to address how you will manage scope, schedule, and budget changes. You will need to do this whether you are the customer, the vendor, or contracting directly with another team member. It's not likely that you will have formal contracts with a project sponsor if they are internal to your organization, but when you do a project plan this can act as the formal agreement on the scope, schedule, and budget of the project (the book, *Cheetah Project Management*, provides guidance on how to create a project plan).

## APPLY IT

For this activity, find standard bid sheets, pricing sheets, and boilerplate contracts for your company that you can use in negotiations. If boilerplate contracts don't exist in your company, search the Internet for standard contracts, bid sheets, and pricing sheets. Find out how your company will be providing these for you, if and when you will be negotiating on their behalf. If you run your own operation, take this time to outline how you will develop your own bid sheets, pricing sheets, and boilerplate contracts for future negotiations. Keep a summary log of what you have discovered. Whether you're using Word, or have a web-based storage

**Table 9.1** Contract Research Worksheet

| Type of Contract | Contracts | Where Located | Who Created |
|---|---|---|---|
| Team member | 1.NDA | 1.HR | 1.IP attorney |
| | 2.Consultant contracts | 2.Purchasing | 2.Corporate counsel |
| Supplier agreements | 1.Use theirs | 1.They have them | 1.They create them. If above 50K, our corporate counsel reviews. |
| Customer contracts | 1.Engagement contract | 1.Sales department | 1.Corporate counsel |
| | 2.Terms of service | 2.Website | 2.Corporate counsel |
| Sponsor agreements | 1.Project Agreement | 1.Product development | 1.Project management office |

system, it is helpful for later reference if you keep a hyperlink document with the results of your research. Table 9.1 provides an example without the hyperlinks.

 **REFLECT**

When you are done with these activities, review the example and see how your work compares. Give a short summary (in three words or less) of your perceptions of the activities. You will remember more about what you did if you can attach a succinct message with some emotion to what you just experienced.

Identify three things you learned by researching contract types.

## Examples from Our Students

### Reflect — What Did I Learn?

- Know where to find what you need and who can assist with contracts.

- The elements that are involved in the agreements.
- The act of "creeping" by attorneys. Contracting teams need to be aware that if the other side's lawyer drafts the first agreement, the terms of the contract will likely be slanted in their client's favor.

### ACT

Identify three things you're going to do differently in your next negotiation based on what you learned by researching contracts.

Since learning is a lifelong pursuit, identify three skills you want to improve because of what you learned in this chapter.

## Examples from Our Students

### Act — What Will I Do Differently?
- Be prepared for the agreements.
- Use the negotiation template for all my meetings.
- Use change-control forms.
- Prepare agreement templates.
- Use of negotiation templates.
- Become more aware of resources available, forms, etc.
- Understand how to control changes.

After you've got the agreement in writing, you have successfully completed the entire negotiation process. All of the steps we have presented will bring you to this final stage fast, and you and the other party can execute the agreement. The next step for you is to practice this negotiation method so that you become proficient in getting what you want, fast. Chapter 10 guides you as you practice going through an entire negotiation from start to finish. Spend some time going through it and making sure you really understand the process by using the examples and templates provided.

*Some feel it's war to negotiate*
*And some outcomes are a matter of fate*
*But it's not war*
*All full of gore*
*Everyone CAN come out feeling great*

*Chapter Ten*

# The Whole Enchilada

*N*ow you have all the pieces to put together your own negotiation production. In this chapter, you'll practice going through a negotiation from the beginning to the end by completing a negotiation prep template. You have seen all these pages and forms in previous chapters.

When you create your own negotiation preparation sheet, make sure all the pages say, "Confidential and Proprietary" — they are for your eyes only. You do not want to share these with the other negotiating parties. But there is one page you will share, which is the negotiation meeting agenda. It is included in the overall template for the sake of completeness. If you will be sending the negotiation meeting agenda to your negotiating counterparts as an e-mail message ahead of time, save it separately and do not send the complete negotiation preparation sheet. To practice, select an upcoming negotiation or a type of a negotiation that you are likely to encounter within the next quarter. Fill out the negotiation prep sheet that you can download from our website at www.cheetahlearning.com. You will find it under the online classes or you can just copy the format in your notebook. You can save this document and use it for preparing for future negotiations as well. We're presenting the blank negotiation prep sheet first, followed by an example of one completed by one of our students (used with permission). Proper preparation is the best way to ensure that your negotiation is successful. As Aristotle said, "Well begun is half done" (Bartlett's, 81).

*Figure 10-1* Negotiation Prep Sheet

Name: _____

Date: _____

## 1.0 Scope

### 1.1 Context — Briefly describe the situation.

_____

_____

_____

### 1.2 Negotiation topic — Briefly describe the negotiation situation.

_____

_____

_____

*(continued on p. 151)*

*Figure 10-1* (continued from p. 150)

## 2.0 Cast of Characters

Identify who will be participating (include yourself in this analysis).

| Participant | Career | Observations/ Indicators | Personality Style | Communication Style | Communication Tactics |
|---|---|---|---|---|---|
| | | | | | |
| | | | | | |
| | | | | | |
| | | | | | |
| | | | | | |
| | | | | | |
| | | | | | |
| | | | | | |
| | | | | | |
| | | | | | |

## 3.0 Setting the Stage

### 3.1 What Do I Want, What Do They Want?

| My Needs | Wants | Why | BATNA | Relationship | Outcome |
|---|---|---|---|---|---|
| | | | | | |

*(continued on p. 152)*

*Figure 10-1* (continued from p. 151)

| Their Needs | Wants | Why | BATNA | Relationship | Outcome |
|---|---|---|---|---|---|
| | | | | | |
| | | | | | |
| | | | | | |

ZOPA:_____

_____

GUAL:_____

_____

*(continued on p. 153)*

*Figure 10-1 (continued from p. 152)*

## 3.2 Negotiation Meeting Checklist

Location: _____ Date: _____

| Participant | Reason for Participation | Phone Number | E-mail | Participation Confirmed |
|---|---|---|---|---|
|  |  |  |  |  |
|  |  |  |  |  |
|  |  |  |  |  |
|  |  |  |  |  |
|  |  |  |  |  |
|  |  |  |  |  |
|  |  |  |  |  |
|  |  |  |  |  |
|  |  |  |  |  |

Start – End Time: _____

### Food

What: _____Who: _____

Contact Information: _____

*(continued on p. 154)*

*Figure 10-1* (continued from p. 153)

When Served:_____

## Restroom Locations

Men _____ Women _____

## Handouts

What is needed? _____

Who is creating? _____

When are they providing them?_____

## Meeting Tools

○ CD Player          ○ Classical Music CDs
○ Yo-yos and Slinkys ○ Mints
○ Clock              ○ Flip Chart
○ Markers            ○ Note Paper
○ Post-Its           ○ Pens
○ Name Tags          ○ Tape
○ Overhead Projector ○ Transparencies
○ LCD Panel          ○ Laptop
○ Phone

## Internet Connection

○ Required           ○ Not required

○ Other: _____

*(continued on p. 155)*

*Figure 10-1* (continued from p. 154)

## 4.0 The Plot

### 4.1 Stress Triggers and Defusers

Identify situations that may come up during this negotiation that have triggered you in the past. Determine how you can make sure they don't trigger you during this negotiation so you can stay calm, relaxed, and detached.

| Stress Triggers | Defusers |
|---|---|
|  |  |
|  |  |
|  |  |
|  |  |

### 4.2 Who Is Wearing What Hat, When?

| Negotiation Stage | When | Hat & Questions/Strategies |
|---|---|---|
| Planning |  |  |
| Introductions |  |  |
| Bargaining |  |  |
| Agreement |  |  |
| Closure |  |  |

*(continued on p. 156)*

*Figure 10-1* (continued from p. 155)

## 5.0 Curtains Up

### 5.1 Money Issues

Identify the money issues that will come up for you and for the other negotiating parties. Identify how you will prepare for these.

| Money Issue | Who | Data Collection (Influence) | Defusers |
|---|---|---|---|
|  |  |  |  |
|  |  |  |  |
|  |  |  |  |

### 5.2 Contracts, Bid Sheets, Pricing Sheets, or Agreements Needed in Negotiation

Identify the legal documentation you will need during the negotiation. Be prepared with the documentation during the meeting so you can formally document and finalize the negotiation.

| Contracts | Where Located | Who Created |
|---|---|---|
| Team member agreements |  |  |
| Supplier agreements |  |  |
| Customer contracts |  |  |
| Sponsor agreements |  |  |

**Figure 10-2** Negotiation Prep Sheet
*Example: Purchasing a House*

Name: *Ted and Alice*

Date: *5/1/2004*

## 1.0 Scope

### 1.1 Context — Briefly describe the situation.
*Alice was recently hired by a company two thousand miles away. Ted, excited about prospects for modeling, is fully behind the move. As part of the compensation package, Alice's new company is paying the closing costs on the sale of her current home and the purchase of her new home. Ted is the one who has to negotiate for the purchase of the new house since Alice is very busy getting settled into her new job.*

*They have found a house in their price range in a neighborhood they both like. It has been on the market for six months. Most other houses in the area have sold in less than two weeks.*

### 1.2 Negotiation Topic — Briefly describe the negotiation situation.
*Ted thinks they can get the house at twenty percent under the price listed based on what the other homes in the neighborhood have sold for in the past six months. It is rumored that the owner may owe more on the house than what it is worth. Ted recently took the class on Cheetah Negotiations and knows he can get a good deal, fast, by adequately preparing.*

## 2.0 Cast of Characters
Identify who will be participating (include yourself in this analysis).

*(continued on p. 158)*

*Figure 10-2* (continued from p. 157)

| Participant | Career | Observations/ Indicators | Personality Style | Communication Style | Communication Tactics |
|---|---|---|---|---|---|
| Ted | Modeling | I am incredibly gorgeous. I like things neat because I care. I live for the moment — that is why I married Alice. | ESFJ | Enough about me, let's talk about what you think about me. | Let's get the topic focused on me. I can be easily swayed with compliments. |
| Alice | Editor | Also very neat — that is why she likes Ken. Reserved and professional — image counts. Aspires to a big career. | INTJ | Get to the point. Not into fluff — wants data. Too busy for chit chat. | Short memos — written communication preferred. Be brief and clear. |
| Percival | Realtor | Befriended Ted very quickly and is now teaching him golf. Lives with his cats and a mysterious "roommate." Must have had a very quiet social life before Ted and Alice moved to town because he now has them over for dinner several times a week. | ESFJ | Very caring — wants to know how everyone is feeling. | Make small talk about his interests — cat, issues with roommate; gossip at golf club. |
| Hazel | Librarian | 55-year-old widow, no children. Owns a big dog. Very quiet, stunning gardens in the yard. | ISFJ | No loud noises. | Complimenting her gardens. Set an appointment to discuss the sale for the home. Meet in the home. |

*(continued on p. 159)*

*Figure 10-2* (continued from p. 158)

## 3.0 Setting the Stage

### 3.1 What Do I Want, What Do They Want?

| My Needs | Wants | Why | BATNA | Relationship | Outcome |
|----------|-------|-----|-------|--------------|---------|
| A home that can accommodate our growing family. We have lots of twinkles and would like lots of little ones. | A nice safe neighborhood with good schools and a big yard, close to the golf course with an easy commute for Alice. | Create a good situation for a family so the stork will deliver. | Get a condo on the golf course. | Low — we will never see Hazel again, but we are becoming good friends with Percival who is also the listing agent and will get both sides of the commission if we purchase Hazel's house. | High — we want this house. It's perfect, just like we are. |

*(continued on p. 160)*

*Figure 10-2* (continued from p. 159)

| Their Needs | Wants | Why | BATNA | Relationship | Outcome |
|---|---|---|---|---|---|
| Hazel's deceased husband, Harry, was a frequent visitor to the golf club. Rumor has it that the hubby took care of all business transactions. His parting words were, "Get a good deal on the house." | Hazel wants the right people in the house (preferably with a green thumb) and to honor Harry's dying wishes. Hazel claims she is moving to Florida to live with her sister. No one recalls her having a sister. Rumor has it she has met someone on the Internet. | Hazel has put a lot of effort into her gardens and wants her legacy to continue. Harry's urn is in the garden and she wants to bury it there as his final resting place. | Stay in her house. | High — she wants to come back and visit Harry. | Low — she's had the house on the market for six months. She's not in a rush to sell it. |

**ZOPA** — *$220K (price of comps)* — *$240K (the amount for which we are qualified).*

**GUAL** — *Not moving off $250K price.*

### 3.2 Negotiation Meeting Checklist

Location: *Hazel's House*          Date: *5/1/2004*
Start – End Time: *2:00 – 3:00 pm*

*(continued on p. 161)*

*Figure 10-2* (continued from p. 160)

| Participant | Reason for Participation | Phone Number | E-mail | Participation Confirmed |
|---|---|---|---|---|
| Ted | He's negotiating on his and Alice's behalf | 555-5555 | Teds@theface.com | Yes |
| Percival | He's the listing agent | 555-5556 | Percival @homes4u.com | Yes |
| Hazel | She is the seller and wants to meet any potential buyer before she entertains bids to be sure that she likes them. | 555-5557 | Hotbabe @yahoo.com | Tentative |

## Food

What: *Finger foods for a garden picnic to celebrate May Day — get Hazel's permission.*

Who: *Percival is getting food.*

When Served: *After a brief tour of the home and grounds.*

## Restroom Locations

Men: *Ground floor — make sure you put the seat down.*

Women: *N/A*

*(continued on p. 162)*

*Figure 10-2* (continued from p. 161)

### Handouts

What is needed? *Ted is bringing the comps on the neighborhood but he has to sell himself first so that Hazel likes the idea of selling the house to them.*

Who is creating? *Me — Ted*

When are they providing them? *Will provide to Percival after the meeting with Hazel.*

### Meeting Tools

| | |
|---|---|
| ⭘ CD Player | ⭘ Classical Music CDs |
| ⭘ Yo-yos and Slinkys | ⭘ Mints |
| ⭘ Clock | ⭘ Flip Chart |
| ⭘ Markers | ⭘ Note Paper |
| ⭘ Post-Its | ⭘ Pens |
| ⭘ Name Tags | ⭘ Tape |
| ⭘ Overhead Projector | ⭘ Transparencies |
| ⭘ LCD Panel | ⭘ Laptop |
| ⭘ Phone | |

### Internet Connection

⭘ Required          ⊗ Not required

⭘ Other: *Make sure clothes are laundered and pressed.*

*(continued on p. 163)*

*Figure 10-2* *(continued from p. 162)*

## 4.0 The Plot

### 4.1 Stress Triggers and Defusers

Identify situations that may come up during this negotiation that have triggered you in the past. Determine how you can make sure

| Stress Triggers | Defusers |
|---|---|
| Dog jumps on my nice clean pants. | Have another pair of the same pants at home so it doesn't matter if these get dirty. |
| Percival gets very fattening food. | Give Percival a list of appropriate food. Eat very small portions of the fattening food. |
| Hazel asks questions about plants and the garden that I can't answer. | I am not familiar with the requirements of this region's gardens since we recently moved from over 2000 miles away, but mention how thrilled we are to learn about how to care for these gardens. Cite the classes I have found at the local community college to learn how to take care of these gardens. |
| Percival starts talking price in front of Hazel and I can tell she is getting upset. | Ask Percival if we can iron out details later. |

they don't trigger you during this negotiation so you can stay calm, relaxed, and detached.

### 4.2 Who Is Wearing What Hat, When

Identify what type of role is needed at various stages of the negotiation and who on your team participating is the most qualified to play that role.

*(continued on p. 164)*

*Figure 10-2* (continued from p. 163)

| Negotiation Stage | When | Hat & Questions/Strategies |
|---|---|---|
| Planning | Several hours after the lunch meeting with Hazel where she meets and really likes Ted.<br><br>Ted says to Percival — I would like to discuss with you an offer on the house, when is a good time to discuss this with you? | White hat — focused on facts and figures. Ted says to Percival, "I would like to discuss with you an offer on the house. When is a good time to discuss this with you?" |
| Introductions | Ted brings up the various factors that impact the money Hazel will get for the house. | Black Hat — Ted bringing up that she owes 80% of the value of the house, that it is priced 20% above market value, and Percival is making 15% commission on the house as the listing and selling agent because of the way he structured the listing contract with an unsuspecting Hazel.<br><br>Ted tells Percival that he met someone who wants to get rid of their condo at the golf course so they have other options. |

*(continued on p. 165)*

*Figure 10-2* (continued from p. 164)

| Negotiation Stage | When | Hat & Questions/Strategies |
|---|---|---|
| Bargaining | First offer — based on comps for comp price — 220K.<br><br>Second offer | Blue Hat — Percival presents offer to Hazel with the data about the sale prices of comparable houses in the neighborhood.<br><br>Red Hat — Hazel is insulted (an anticipated worst case response)<br><br>Green Hat — Ted proposes to Percival that they cover all closing costs, including commission at the lower price. This means that Hazel walks away with just about as much money as if she gets full price. Percival gets a lower commission.<br><br>Blue Hat — Percival presents second offer to cover all closing costs and explains impact on the final amount she walks away with. |
| Agreement | Finalizing agreement | Percival uses real estate agreement forms to finalize agreement. |
| Closure | Closing on deal | Deal is finalized through the escrow company. |

## 5.0 Curtains Up

### 5.1 Money Issues

Identify the money issues that will come up for you and for the other negotiating parties. Identify how you will prepare for these.

*(continued on p. 166)*

*Figure 10-2* (continued from p. 165)

### 5.2 Contracts, Bid Sheets, Pricing Sheets, or Agreements Needed in Negotiation

Identify the legal documentation you will need during the negotiation. Be prepared with the documentation during the meeting so you can formally document and finalize the negotiation.

| Money Issue | Who | Data Collection (Influence) | Defusers |
|---|---|---|---|
| Real estate commission | Percival | Find out total commission | Find out what is standard for commissions when the realtor is getting both the listing and the sales commission. |
| Value of the home | Hazel | The comps and the fact that there have been no offers in six months | Focus on what Hazel will walk away with after all closing costs with the original contract. |
| Paying all the closing costs | Alice | Find out if there is a cap on the closing costs for the house. | Review the employment contract. |

| Contracts | Where Located | Who Created |
|---|---|---|
| Offer contract | Real estate office | Standard real estate contract |
| Contract acceptance | Real estate office | Standard real estate contract |
| Closing documents | Escrow company | Escrow company follows laws of the state |

*(continued on p. 167)*

*Figure 10-2* *(continued from p. 166)*

**Additional Notes**

_____

_____

_____

_____

_____

_____

_____

 **REFLECT**

When you are done with these activities, review the example and see how your work compares. Give a short summary (in three words or less) of your perceptions of the activities. You will remember more about what you did if you can attach a succinct message with some emotion to what you just experienced.

Identify three things you learned by completing a negotiation prep sheet.

**Examples from Our Students**

Reflect — What Did I Learn?

- I learned that using the forms from the class will prepare me for my next negotiation.

- I am better prepared for the negative responses from the other parties involved now that I understand their personalities, want and needs, and roles.
- The process helps me to determine who needs to be included in the negotiation so that a resolution can occur.
- Permission questions can be a great tool.

## ACT

Identify three things you're going to do differently in your next negotiation based on what you learned by filling out a negotiation prep sheet.

Since learning is a lifelong pursuit, identify three skills you want to improve because of what you learned in this chapter.

### Examples from Our Students

#### Act — What Will I Do Differently?

- I want to do a better job of preparation — be more honest with myself and do the work even when it feels distasteful.
- Try where possible to mentally relax in tension-filled situations. Employ tension management techniques prior to a negotiation meeting. Also, recommend these strategies to my fellow team members.
- In an effort to manage people's time effectively, I will ensure in advance that the right people or appropriate delegates will be attending any negotiation meeting I take part in organizing.
- Start with the end in mind.
- Mentally walk through the entire process to better prepare for closure and to anticipate needs.
- Preparation; ideally I would like to bring more structure to how I prepare for a negotiation, as was described in this course. Issue identification, position setting, priority ranking,

and execution are all key areas within negotiation management I need to improve upon.

- Be prepared and predetermine roles of participants to make sure that I have the appropriate people involved.
- Plan, plan, plan. And if faced with an unscheduled negotiation, ask to defer the meeting until a prep sheet and agenda can be developed.
- Practice relaxation techniques through diet and exercise. Use breathing techniques during tense negotiations.

# Conclusion

*I*f you read and follow the steps outlined in this book, you have the ability to get what you want, fast. As we discussed, the best way to achieve this is to help others get what they want. You can do this by preparing properly, focusing on treating others fairly, and remembering to remain as objective and detached as possible. Learn and practice the process and use it in your daily life. Implementing the steps we have outlined here will ensure you rapid success in any negotiation situation. Be clear, fair, and firm, and you will negotiate successfully for what you want, fast!

# Feelings
# and Needs

## CENTER FOR NON-VIOLENT COMMUNICATIONS (WWW.CNVC.ORG)
## FEELINGS AND NEEDS STATEMENTS

When negotiating, it may help to use this list to capture the nuance of your feelings and/or needs. Then you will have far better success with achieving the goal of keeping all parties focused on objectives rather than positions and can more easily defuse harmful negotiation tactics.

The listing begins on the following page.

# FEELINGS EXPERIENCED WHEN YOUR NEEDS ARE SATISFIED

## Affectionate
compassionate
friendly
loving
open-hearted
sympathetic
tender
warm

## Confident
empowered
open
proud
safe
secure

## Engaged
absorbed
alert
curious
engrossed
enchanted
entranced
fascinated
interested
intrigued
involved
spellbound
stimulated

## Inspired
amazed
awed
wonder

## Excited
amazed
animated
ardent
aroused
astonished
dazzled
eager
energetic
enthusiastic
giddy
invigorated
lively
passionate
surprised
vibrant

## Exhilarated
blissful
ecstatic
elated
enthralled
exuberant
radiant
rapturous
thrilled

## Grateful
appreciative
moved
thankful
touched

## Hopeful
expectant
encouraged
optimistic

## Joyful
amused
delighted
glad
happy
jubilant
pleased
tickled

## Peaceful
calm
clear-headed
comfortable
centered
content
equanimous
fulfilled
mellow
quiet
relaxed

relieved
satisfied
serene
still
tranquil

trusting

**Refreshed**
enlivened
rejuvenated

renewed
rested
restored
revived

# FEELINGS EXPERIENCED WHEN YOUR NEEDS ARE NOT SATISFIED

**Afraid**
apprehensive
dread
foreboding
frightened
mistrustful
panicked
petrified
scared
suspicious
terrified
wary
worried

**Annoyed**
aggravated
dismayed
disgruntled
displeased
exasperated
frustrated
impatient
irritated
irked

**Angry**
enraged
furious
incensed
indignant
irate
livid
outraged
resentful

**Aversion**
animosity
appalled
contempt
disgusted
dislike
hate
horrified
hostile
repulsed

**Confused**
ambivalent
baffled

bewildered
dazed
hesitant
lost
mystified
perplexed
puzzled
torn

**Disconnected**
alienated
aloof
apathetic
bored
cold
detached
distant
distracted
indifferent
numb
removed
uninterested
withdrawn

### Disquiet

agitated
alarmed
discombobulated
disconcerted
disturbed
perturbed
rattled
restless
shocked
startled
surprised
troubled
turbulent
turmoil
uncomfortable
uneasy
unnerved
unsettled
upset

### Embarrassed

ashamed
chagrined
flustered
guilty
mortified
self-conscious

### Fatigue

beat
burnt out
depleted
exhausted
lethargic
listless
sleepy
tired
weary
worn out

### Pain

agony
anguished
bereaved
devastated
grief
heartbroken
hurt
lonely
miserable
regretful
remorseful

### Sad

depressed
dejected
despair
despondent
disappointed
discouraged
disheartened

forlorn
gloomy
heavy-hearted
hopeless
melancholy
unhappy
wretched

### Tense

anxious
cranky
distressed
distraught
edgy
fidgety
frazzled
irritable
jittery
nervous
overwhelmed
restless
stressed out

### Vulnerable

fragile
guarded
helpless
insecure
leery
reserved
sensitive
shaky

**Yearning**
envious
jealous

longing
nostalgic
pining

wistful

## NEEDS INVENTORY

**Connection**
acceptance
affection
appreciation
belonging
cooperation
communication
closeness
community
companionship
compassion
consideration
consistency
empathy
inclusion
intimacy
love
mutuality
nurturing
respect/self-respect
safety
security
stability
support
to know and be
   known

to see and be seen
to understand and
   be understood
trust
warmth

**Honesty**
authenticity
integrity
presence

**Play**
joy
humor

**Peace**
beauty
communion
ease
equality
harmony
inspiration
order

**Physical Well-Being**
air
food
movement/
   exercise
rest/sleep
sexual expression
safety
shelter
touch
water

**Meaning**
awareness
celebration of life
challenge
clarity
competence
consciousness
contribution
creativity
discovery
efficacy
effectiveness
growth
hope

learning
mourning
participation
purpose
self-expression
stimulation
to matter
understanding

## Autonomy

choice
freedom
independence
space
spontaneity

# Works Cited

Barrett, E. Thorpe. 2000, 3rd ed. *Write your own business contracts: What your attorney won't tell you.* Grants Pass, OR: Oasis.

Bartlett, John (comp). 2002. *Bartlett's familiar quotations.* New York: Little, Brown and Company.

Brinkman, Rick. 1994. *Dealing with people you can't stand.* New York: McGraw-Hill.

Cialdini, Robert B., PhD. 1998, rev. ed. *Influence: The psychology of persuasion* New York: Perennial Currents.

Cohen, Allan R., and David L. Bradford. 1991, rev. ed. *Influence without authority.* Hoboken, NJ: Wiley.

Crum, Thomas F. 1998. *The magic of conflict: Turning a life of work into a work of art.* New York: Touchstone.

De Bono, Edward. 1999, rev. ed. *Six thinking hats*. New York: Back Bay Books.

Dimitrius, Jo-Ellan, and Mark C. Mazzarella. 1999. *Reading people: How to understand people and predict their behavior — anytime, anyplace.* New York: Ballantine Books.

Donaldson, Michael C., et al. 1996. *Negotiating for dummies.* New York: For Dummies.

Fisher, Roger, William Ury, and Bruce Patton. 1991. *Getting to yes: Negotiating agreement without giving in.* New York: Penguin Books.

Frey, Phillis H., and Martin A. Frey. 2000. *Essentials of contract law.* Albany, NY: Delmar Learning.

Hindle, Tim. 1999. *Negotiating skills (Essential managers).* New York: DK Publishing, Inc.

Kiyosaki, Robert T., and Sharon L. Lechter. 2000. *Rich dad, poor dad: What the rich teach their kids about money—that the poor and middle class do not!* New York: Warner Business Books.

Labrosse, Michelle, PMP. 2004. *Cheetah project management.* Nevada: MAKLAF PRESS.

Lewicki, Roy J. 1996. *Think before you speak: A complete guide to strategic negotiation.* Hoboken, NJ: Wiley.

Lieberman, David J. 1999. *Never be lied to again: How to get the truth in 5 minutes or less in any conversation or situation.* New York: St. Martin's Griffin.

Lieberman, David J. 2000. *Get anyone to do anything: Never feel powerless again—with psychological secrets to control and influence every situation.* New York: St. Martin's Press.

McMains, Michael, J, and Wayman C. Mullins. 2001. *Crisis negotiations: Managing critical incidents and hostage situations in law enforcement and corrections.* Cincinnati: Anderson Publishing.

Myers, Isabel, and Katharine Briggs. 1998, 3rd ed. *Myers-Briggs type indicator® (MBTI).* California: Consulting Psychologists Press.

Rosenberg, Marshall B. and Lucy Leu. 2003, 2nd ed. *Nonviolent communication, a language of life: Create your life, your relationships, and your world in harmony with your values.* California: PuddleDancer Press.

Shell, G. Richard. 2000. *Bargaining for advantage: Negotiation strategies for reasonable people.* New York: Penguin Books.

Tieger, Paul, and Barbara Barron-Tieger. 1999. *The art of speed reading people: How to size people up and speak their language.* New York: Little, Brown and Company.

Tieger, Paul E., and Barbara Barron-Tieger. 2001. *Do what you are: Discover the perfect career for you through the secrets of personality type.* New York: Little, Brown and Company.

Tingley, Judith C. 2000. *The power of indirect influence.* New York: American Management Association.

Ury, William. 1993. *Getting past no: Negotiating your way from confrontation to cooperation.* New York: Bantam Books.

# Index

strengths and blind spots, 15–16

relations with ENTP per-
sonality, 22t
vitamin B, 59

**W**

walking, as exercise, 60
wants *versus* needs, 44
white hat (leader role), 64,
68t, 91t
"why" of negotiation, 44–45
win-win, negotiation as, 82
worksheets
contract research,
144–45, 145t
permission-based ques-
tions, 91t
*Write Your Own Business Con-
tracts* (Barrett),
141–42, 181
written word, as commit-
ment tool, 98

**Y**

yellow hat (good cop role),
67, 68t, 91t

**Z**

ZOPA (zone of possible
agreement)
anchoring, 85–86
defined, 46
determining, 84
employee pay raise nego-
tiation example,
48f

## About the Author

# Michelle LaBrosse

*M*ichelle LaBrosse has a full-figure personality. She is a rocket scientist — yes, you read that right — a bona fide rocket scientist. When she woke up and realized she no longer enjoyed being a rocket scientist but instead had a deep and genuine love of learning (and laughing), she set out on a new path — to bring the love and joy of learning to professionals. Michelle found that most traditional educational environments sucked the life force out of people's desire to learn — especially her own. Being into research (reference her early career as a rocket scientist), she began to study how to make learning faster, easier, and a lot more fun.

Using current methods on accelerated learning, project management, and negotiations, LaBrosse has grown her company, Cheetah Learning, into the profitable, market leader in Project Management training in four years. So how did Michelle generate this level of success so quickly in a market in recession? Well, it certainly did not come from behaving the way "good girls" do. Says LaBrosse: "We're easy, we're fun, and we're fast."

Michelle has a B.S. in Aerospace Engineering from Syracuse University, an M.S. in Mechanical Engineering from University of Dayton, and is currently enrolled in Harvard Business School's three-year Owner President Management program for entrepreneurs. Michelle was profiled in the book, *Rich Dad's Success Stories*, by Robert Kiyosaki and is a member of the Women President's Organization.

# Linda Lansky

*L*inda Lansky is an integral part of the Cheetah Learning Team. She is a certified coach for the Cheetah Exam Prep for the PMP. Linda's project management experience comes from over twenty years in Information Technology & Quality Management in the semiconductor industry. Linda is a member of the American Society for Training and Development (ASTD), PMI and received her training certificate from Langevin Learning Services. Linda is the lead designer on the creative collaboration team for the development of new Cheetah Learning courses. Back at her ranch in northern California, Linda enjoys her horses, cattle, dogs, family, and a home vineyard and fledgling winery — not necessarily in that order.

# Cheetah Negotiations Online Course

## Communicate Your Way to Success

Would you like to improve your day to day effectiveness as a Project Manager with Cheetah negotiation strategies and techniques? This course will help you negotiate in the many situations that are all in a day's work. Communicate more effectively with team members, sponsors, stakeholders, functional managers, customers and vendors. You'll also experience a negotiation styles assessment that will help you understand your negotiating strengths and challenges.

## Course Details

| | |
|---|---|
| **Credit -** | 20 PDUs, 2.0 CEUs |
| **Cost -** | $395 |
| **Duration -** | 20 hours (you will have eight weeks to access the online content and inter-act with your instructor) |
| **Course Material -** | All provided online |
| **Course Location -** | Online |
| **Accreditation -** | PMI® R.E.P., IACET |

**Registration** www.cheetahpm.com or (800) 246-9106

CHEETAH™ Project Management

# Visit Our Website for More Ways to Expand Your Success Story Fast

*Exam Preparation*

*Project Management Training*

*Free Downloads*

CHEETAH LEARNING®
Knowledge, Confidence, Reliability

www.cheetahlearning.com

MAKLAF
PRESS